Acknowledgements

Unlocking The Door was first published in 2006 and was written by Ruth Adams and Jan Harney. Ruth worked for Activate as the National Co-ordinator for almost 30 years and was the amazing driving force behind many training courses, national speaking tours, beautiful inspiring magazines and conferences.

Jan was Activate's National Development Officer for eight years and the creative, fun-filled spark in the team. We are eternally grateful for their work for Activate and all those who they brought to Jesus over the years.

Activate Your Life is now a team of volunteers who continue to develop and encourage friendship evangelism. We love the original book and are delighted to have the opportunity to update it with new references and fresh stories of God's love in action. Thank you to all those who were brave enough to share their adventures and heartaches. To Fiona Castle, our president, and to the whole Dream Team and Leadership Team who put in so much work and always have a lot of fun together - we appreciate you!

The editorial team:
Rhiannon Goulding
Fiona Castle
Caroline Middleton
Sarah McKerney
Mandy Catto
Julie McQuoid

activate your life
women actively sharing god's love

What's inside?

Why Did You Pick Up This Book?

What Have You Got In The House?

Inspiration

Why did **you** pick up this book?

Perhaps you have a heart to reach out to someone close to you and you want to know where to start. Do you feel that you lack the confidence or skills to be effective? Maybe it is years since you had an authentic conversation about faith that led someone closer to Jesus.

We believe that you are just the sort of person whom God chooses to build His kingdom. You may not believe you are an evangelist; you might even worry about getting it wrong. This book will convince you that the smallest efforts you make to connect with other people can make an impact beyond anything you expect or dream about. Let God surprise you with the results.

A few months ago I watched as my good friend Carol found Jesus, whilst sitting on the sofa in my lounge. After many years of friendship, many invitations, rejections, conversations and shared heartaches and joys, she opened up and began exploring the concept of faith in Jesus. When she heard and understood for the first time that life in all its fullness and eternal happiness was all about accepting Jesus, she asked, 'Is it really that simple? I just have to believe and trust him'.

Then as the conversation continued and others spoke, I watched her face change and her eyes fill up. No one had yet told her about the Holy Spirit but she said that as she said 'yes', she felt a warm glow pouring inside her from head to toe. As the angels in heaven rejoiced, I could see in her face that she was a new person. Changed for eternity. There is nothing quite like watching a good friend step closer to Jesus.

This book is dedicated to Carol, and to our other friends. That it might inspire, resource and encourage more of us to speak out, share, love and bring others closer to him.

'**Evangelism is not a professional job for a few trained men,** but is instead the unrelenting possibility of every person who belongs to the company of Jesus.'

Elton Trueblood

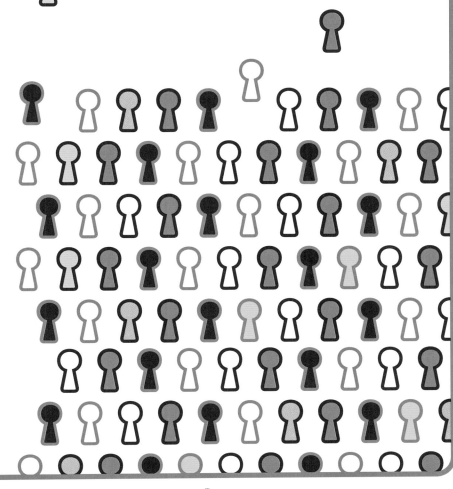

Why do we need **another** evangelism resource?

Christians are busy people.

Often we're so busy going to meetings that we're in danger of being out of touch with the world outside which has little interest in the church or its activities.

There are plenty of evangelistic resources available, but most assume that Christians have a wide circle of contacts to invite to the various courses on offer. Yet, our research shows that the majority of Christians - and church leaders - have few, if any, close friends outside their church circles. A church in South West England with 500 members announced the launch of a 'Christianity Explored' course with many encouragments for people to invite their friends. One month later, eight people showed up, five of them were already regular church members. A professor at a Bible College said recently, "Alpha? Who on earth would I invite? Where do you meet people who are non-believers?". A church deacon was heard saying – "I do not have any friends outside my church circle, not even one. All my activities are church centred: except for my badminton group, but I don't really speak to anyone there."

So, this is where this book will start, helping Christians build meaningful relationships with those in their 'circle of influence' whether this is in the workplace, the home, or leisure activities.

Steps to Christ

We will start at Step 1 and through a wide variety of practical, natural and creative activities provide a variety of ideas which ensure there are opportunities for every Christian to see how they can be salt and light, by building up meaningful relationships with those around them.

We encourage you to get alongside and build relationships with people who have little or no knowledge of God. When Christians get to know people and build relationships with them, they effectively take people from steps 1 and 2, onto step 3 – Contact with Christians. The person has moved a step up the staircase before you begin to share anything. Then we pray that, through positive contact with Christians, those within our circle of influence will begin to be intrigued and interested in Jesus (step 4), and eventually decide to investigate Jesus (step 5). It is at this stage we pray that they will be receptive to investigate the Christian faith further.

Fifty years ago the great Christian author, C.S. Lewis finished putting together his classic work, 'Mere Christianity.'

'The world does not consist of 100% Christians and 100% non-Christians', he wrote. 'There are people who are slowly ceasing to be Christians but who still call themselves by that name. There are other people who are slowly becoming Christians though they do not yet call themselves so. There are people who do not accept the full Christian doctrine about Christ but who are so strongly attracted by him that they are his in a much deeper sense than they themselves understand. There are people in other religions who are being led by God's secret influence to concentrate on those parts of their religion which are in agreement with Christianity and who thus belong to Christ without knowing it'.

Lewis was pointing out something he believed to be plainly obvious, not only from his experience of life, but also from his reading of the words of Jesus – things just aren't that black and white. Shorthand terms like Christian and non-Christian may at first appear useful but once you dig a little deeper you soon realise that they can cause us to miss the point entirely.

As far as Jesus was concerned, it is evident that it wasn't how close someone was to him at any given

The Engel Scale, from:
**'What's gone wrong
with the harvest'**
J F Engel and W H Norton

10 COMMITMENT TO CHRIST

9 ACCEPTANCE OF IMPLICATIONS

8 UNDERSTAND THE IMPLICATIONS

7 ACCEPTANCE OF CHRISTIAN TRUTH

6 GRASP THE TRUTH ABOUT JESUS

5 DECIDE TO INVESTIGATE JESUS

4 INTEREST IN CHRIST

3 CONTACT WITH CHRISTIANS

2 SOME AWARENESS OF GOD

NO AWARENESS OF GOD

stage in their life that mattered, as much as the direction in which they were travelling. Judas, for example, shared some of Jesus' most intimate moments; he was one of the inner community of twelve, right up until the Last Supper. For anyone looking in from the outside his relationship with Jesus would have appeared, superficially at least, cosy and close. But, begin to scratch away the surface and you would have soon discovered that he was heading away from Jesus rather than being drawn closer – he was travelling in the wrong direction. In the end only God knows where anyone really stands with him.

The bridge th

'Every few hundred years throughout Western history a sharp transformation occurs. In a matter of decades society rearranges itself – its world view, its basic values, its social and political structures, its art, its key institutions. Fifty years later a new world exists, and people born into that world cannot even imagine the world into which their grandparents were born. Our age is such a transformation'

Peter Drucker

Few would disagree with this statement, as we consider the changes which have occurred in our society over the past few decades. Changes, which for many Christians have made it increasingly difficult to relate their faith with the world around them.

This photograph of a bridge in Honduras, South America is taken from National Geographic magazine. The little Lego–like structure in the front is actually a bridge that used to span the river. In 1998, Hurricane Mitch hit Honduras and 100 inches of rainfall fell in five days. In Honduras, that amount of rain is not unusual

over six or twelve months, but in five days the effect was catastrophic. As you can see, the hurricane caused devastation to the landscape, and the riverbed actually moved.

When change is gradual, we hardly notice it, a bit like 100 inches of rain in a year but when it happens as quickly as it has over recent years, the effect is more like 100 inches of rainfall in five days.

Is this photograph an illustration of us as Christians or of the church? We stand firm no matter what happens around us, but have we ceased to be effective, a little like the bridge, which is now only a tourist

at didn't move

attraction. The Japanese engineers who built the bridge were delighted that it withstood the hurricane, but it's no longer fulfilling its purpose, because the river is somewhere else.

The structures which we have in place may be strong and unmovable but are they fulfiling the purpose they were created for?

The picture is a challenge for us to have a look at some of the structures that we have in place in the Christian world, because what was effective evangelism in the past may well be ineffective now because of the major changes in culture that we've seen over the last few decades.

Street corner evangelism, with Bible verses being loudly spoken out to strangers, was once considered the only way to do evangelism. And crusades with a famous speaker arriving from abroad, filling a stadium for a one-week series of talks was very popular. Coffee bars with live music and hot drinks to rival pubs were considered very fashionable. In their day, they had their place.

And today? We need to listen to God and be working where God is working, not stuck in the past, hanging on to our safe, tried and tested structures, but going with the flow of where God's river is currently flowing.

Christians
in Hiding

(Church as an Alien Institution)

In the course of her work as a reporter, Emma had to meet a photographer for an assignment at a well-known restaurant. They had never met before, but the conversation flowed easily. Before long, discussion about glamour models had turned to religion and the church, and James was flabbergasted to discover that Emma, an attractive 25 year old, was a Christian. He confessed he had never before in his 41 years, met anyone who 'believed all that stuff'. Over a bottle of champagne their conversation continued until closing time.

Emma was working on what might be considered by some Christians to be a 'downmarket' Sunday newspaper, but in the course of her work meets people who have often never spoken to a 'real' Christian before. Should this surprise us?

In the film 'Salmon Fishing in the Yemen' the main character, played by Ewan McGregor, watches some Muslims praying and comments – "I don't know anyone who goes to church now. We have moved on from religion. Instead of going to church,

which would never occur to us, we go to Tescos together on Sundays."

Rev Joanna Jepson, a vicar from Chester says, "The church is now an alien institution for the bulk of my generation, the iGeneration". She says, "During time spent as a barmaid and youth worker among victims of drug abuse I tried to get my mates to come to church with me, yet when one of them actually came I had to question the effectiveness of my plan. Scott was a punk who squatted in barns and ate speed and ice cream. He agreed to come to a service with me and did so for some weeks, until it was evident he was in danger of being turned into a middle-class Christian. He believed what he heard but the Church didn't allow him to find language to express his growing spirituality. And I felt uneasy watching punk-boy head towards having to drain his hair of colour, lose the piercings and join the rows of homogenised, beige and navy Christians.

Out of frustrations like this I, and others, have been provoked to go into ordained ministry in the hope of enabling those on the fringes to find a place of belonging. The Church should not apologise for who we are and the truth that shapes our identity. But the language we use to express those things needs to speak to, rather than alienate, those who have grown up rarely crossing the threshold of the Church".

This sense of alienation is also mentioned by George Lings (Church Army - 'Encounters on the Edge' booklet - Living Proof).

"To the unchurched, church is what some others do. It is noticed sadly, in their terms, not only as an alien and expensive building I wouldn't know what to do in, worse, it's occupied by people I wouldn't be seen dead with. To them, Church is about internal bickering over issues no-one else cares about, inconsistent lives that make claims in ridiculous words, led by people who don't know what they believe and are probably not to be trusted with other people's children."

Those of us, like Emma and Joanna, who want to help James and Scott and others like them find the reality of faith in Jesus, want to spark conversations and friendships, which will in turn give rise to new ways of living and communicating our faith in this changing world.

What about the church? So often we get stuck in the mindset of wanting to bring people to church. But church is not often the best place to start.

The church can often be outspoken in pride about the fact that we are still here – in spite of all the catastrophes that have threatened our existence. But are we still fulfilling our original brief?

William Temple said, "The church is the only organization in the world that exists for the benefit of its non-members." Does that sound like your church?

In the UK 2011 census nearly 60% of people claimed to be Christian, yet only a small percentage of them are sitting in church on a regular basis; in some areas church attendance is 5%. Reasons might include apathy, overwork and needing a rest on Sundays, dislike of worship styles, or a host of other reasons. Some people have felt hurt

> '**Even if 80 percent of the population of a country are Christian believers,** they will have almost no cultural influence if the Christians do not live in cultural centres and work in culture-forging fields such as academia, publishing, media, entertainment, and the arts. The assumption that society will improve simply because more Christian believers are present is no longer valid.'
>
> **Tim Keller**

or let down by the church in the past. Others may be put off by the media portrayal of the establishment. Many people only understand the Christian faith in terms of what they hear on the news, see on the latest soap or watch on a TV programme. If they have never been inside a church, a fact of life for a huge percentage of the country, the television is the main source of information for them. Many like James, may never have even spoken to a 'real' Christian.

A survey from 2009 found that only 5% of people could name all of the ten commandments, and 16% couldn't remember even one. This illustrates well the fact that we need to start where people are, not where we want them to be. So often people have far less understanding than we realise of the basics of the Christian faith that we take for granted.

If we continue to stay in our safe ghettos and holy huddles, it's not surprising that the 'life in all its fulness' which Jesus promised, won't be conveyed to those outside the church.

Unchurched / De-churched

In his booklet 'Living Proof – a new way of being church?' George Lings of the Church Army offers some helpful definitions to help us engage more effectively with people outside the church by identifying their reasons for being there:

Who Are the De-churched?

The de-churched include those sometimes called 'the lapsed'. They may have dropped out of a church in a house move, or because of a change of vicar, or when work patterns changed. Further out on the fringes of the de-churched are many who went to Sunday school or a youth group, they were married in church, or they are among the 28% who had a child baptized. They would at least consider going to church at Christmas and hope to survive the experience.

Yet further out are the people whose parents had those kinds of links and those with pressures from the extended family to seek baptism of a child. These are those who come back to faith, or who find a substance where previously there was only the shadow, through today's forms of evangelism and pastoral care. In many cases, someone in the family or friendship group has been praying for them – perhaps for years.

Who are the Unchurched?

Here there is no history of regular church attendance for three or four previous generations. There is no-one living in the extended family for whom this is part of normal life. No one prays for them by name. This is a major group in urban society and it is frighteningly possible that we are blind in practice, and in tactics, to their existence.

Not even Unchurched but Non-churched

While the distinction between de-churched and unchurched has been made and is used, it is perhaps better to choose language that makes the contrast yet starker for such is the difference between them. George Lings would suggest using the term 'non-churched' as 'unchurched' could easily imply that once this category of people were churched and they somehow lost that connection. This is neither true nor helpful, and it is interesting that both terms unchurched and de-churched

betray a cast of mind that assumes that all people are somehow our people.

It would be helpful in this major rethink of a vast mission need to recognize that groups which are profoundly non-churched present a cultural group, more than simply a neighbourhood. What defines them is not their address but their attitudes.

All our historical associations with neighbourhood, invite mission responses which are merely extensions of past patterns of working with those we fondly term 'our people'. We then invite them in a variety of ways to come and join us. The social and mission reality is that this enormous sector of society are not 'our people' – they haven't been in living memory, nor do they want to be. Such language is alienating and patronising.

The reality is all the more significant when in the majority of cases, the group one is talking about represents, not some obscure minority group, but arguably the majority of inhabitants in all our industrial cities.

The Parable of the sower

Creative Idea

Read together Matthew 13 vs 1-9 (The Parable of the sower)

As the leader reads, you might want to have paper and pens available and take the opportunity to draw the four different areas into an image of a field as you listen.

Jesus liked to talk through stories. He shared his message through parables - earthly stories with a heavenly meaning. These picture stories would have been readily available to those listening to him; they would have been

Parables- 'extended similes' that include the phrase 'is like' somewhere in the middle.

able to picture exactly the field and the farmer sowing his seeds with a scattering action. In each verse there is a different outcome to the seed that the farmer has sown. So, perhaps, this parable is more about the soil than the sower!

Q Why do you think Jesus told parables when the people gathered to listen and learn from him? Did he want to explain in clear contemporary pictures?

Q Or, looking at vs 11 – 17, did he feel he had to hide the truth from those with hardened hearts who were not listening?

This parable apppears in the gospels of Matthew, Mark and Luke.

A half-hearted approach to God's word will not yield you much good. As we look at this parable of Jesus take the effort to meditate on the meaning. If we assume that we already know all there is to know about the parables we will not receive much. Make it your prayer that God will open your eyes to understand and your heart to perceive the truths He has in store for you from His Word.

Q Why would a farmer allow precious seed to land on the path, or rocks, or among thorns? Is he an irresponsible farmer scattering seeds at random? It is helpful to try and picture the type of ground that was common in Jesus' day, a rough hardened ground without formal borders or fences. Fertile ground was surrounded by and interspersed with paths and clumps of weeds. If the farmer wanted seeds to fall on good soil then he inevitably had to spread seeds to the whole area. We are called too, not to be prejudiced or judgmental in who we make connections with and speak about our faith to. Our job is to speak naturally and make the most of any opportunity.

Read vs Matt 13:18-23.
The path - the seeds here were
eaten by birds.

The four types of listeners may be described as hard-hearted, shallow-hearted, half-hearted, and whole-hearted.

Q Why is it that some people don't understand the message? Are their hearts hardened or do we sometimes fail to explain and communicate in a helpful and clear way? Does jargon or tradition sometimes blur the message of Jesus' love and forgiveness to your friends?

Jesus does not go on to explain what the path might mean but he does talk about who the birds are in v19. Give some practical examples of how Satan can steal the word from hearts.

The rocky place. The seeds did spring up and begin to grow but the roots could not go deep as the soil was so shallow. Read verses 5 and 6 as well as verses 20 and 21. There was joy at the beginning but it was overtaken by other concerns, in particular trouble or persecution because of faith.

Q Do we do enough to support new believers or those earnestly seeking the first few times they come to church?

The Christian life is designed to be enjoyed with others. Jesus invested much of His ministry with 12 disciples as His closest friends. He likewise calls us to live in community with one another. And if we are connected and honest with one another then we can support and pray for each other when trouble and persecution come.

> The New Testament has over 50 "one another" verses that refer to loving one another, serving one another, encouraging one another, and praying for one another. Each of these commands requires relationships with other Christians.

Q What does persecution look like for us today? We may face scorn, rejection and loneliness and we can ask for God's strength to persevere. Let's remember our Christian sisters and brothers who face steeper challenges. An article in the Spectator tells us that between 2006 and 2010 Christians faced some sort of discrimination in 139 nations, which is almost three quarters of all the countries on earth! According to the Centre for the Study of Global Christianity an average of 100,000 Christians have been killed in a 'situation of witness' each year for the past decade. Take a moment to pray for those facing prison or death today.

So how can we stand strong through any types of persecution? Having Christian friends is one part of the solution but having deep roots is the key.

Q How can we be rooted deeply in Christ Jesus? **Look up Ephesians 3 vs 16-19**. Being rooted in love is the key.

Vs 6 - the thorns

Q What are some of the thorns that people face in the world today?

Jesus specifically mentions two: the worries of this life and the deceitfulness of wealth.

Q Can you think of people you know who may have been initially enthusiastic about embracing faith, then fell away when worry overtook them? Our lives today could easily be dominated by worry and dread.

Q How can we keep our thoughts about the future in a positive perspective? Look up Matthew 6 vs 25-34. Jesus tells us that our Heavenly Father knows all our needs and that He will give us all we need.

Q Why is wealth deceitful? 1 Timothy 6: 6-19 shows us that we cannot trust in money, our trust must be in God.

Q Why couldn't those who received the word with joy stay faithful? (8:13)

Read Colossians 2: 6-8. What does this say about deepening the roots of your faith?

Good ground - The Bible here talks about bearing fruit with patience. Why do we need patience to bear fruit? Can you give some examples of fruit bearing?

Jesus describes the level of fruitfulness as thirtyfold, sixtyfold, and a hundredfold. This is not to be confused, as it often is, with 30%, 60%, and 100%. If a man invests £100 and makes 100%, he will end up with £200. But the man who invests £100 and makes a hundredfold has made another £10,000. Jesus is talking about abundant extravagant fruit!

We know that when Jesus explained this parable he was talking about different sets of people and how they reacted when they initially heard His message. But we can think of this in relation to ourselves too.

Q What kind of soil do you most resemble right now? What worries or temptations have hindered your growth as a Christian recently? Are joy, perseverance and fruitfulness part of your life?

Music
This is a helpful short video on the passage www.youtube.com/ watch?v=E0avbJ68nBs

Our Challenge as Christians

While the words 'religion' and 'church' might have negative connotations for some people, the word 'spirituality' is viewed positively by most of the population and our society has never been more interested in 'spirituality' than it is today. The problem for us is that spiritual searchers aren't looking to Christians or the church for the answers to their questions, as they often don't feel we have anything to offer, but are turning to publications like the increasingly popular monthly women's magazine 'Spirit & Destiny'. Offering to cater for the 'essential, inner, spiritual you' this magazine appeals to the search people have for meaning by offering a whole range of alternative therapies.

This search for meaning is highlighted by a comment by David Beckham a while ago, 'I want my baby to be christened, but I don't know into what religion yet'.

The response to this by many Christians is to quietly laugh at his lack of understanding. However, perhaps others believe valuable insight into people's spiritual state can be gleaned from this kind of moment. David Coffey suggests 'our challenge as Christians is to find ways of relating to the bewildering spirituality of our times. People may appear superstitious but their questions are often a starting point that will lead them to a genuine encounter with Jesus Christ'.* How willing are we to engage with the spiritual searchers who are almost certainly living and working around us?

One difficulty is that what we're doing now has become monochrome, reaching only one part of the community. Diversity is God-given, yet we've narrowed things down and tend to treat everyone the same. For hundreds of years we've sent missionaries overseas and taken it for granted that their first task would be learning the language of the country they're going to. Yet, today, in Britain there are many different cultural languages being spoken and we need a different language to reach each group of people. There is no one language that is better than another but if we are not speaking the same language as the people around us, they won't understand what we're talking about.

John Drane has identified seven lifestyle groups which we need to connect with if we are to reach

*David Coffey - Address to the Baptist Assembly, 2002

"The greatest compliment that was ever paid me was when one asked me what I thought, and attended to my answer.'

David Thoreau

significant groups of people in our society.

1 Traditionalists

2 Corporate achievers

3 Desperate poor

4 Spiritual searchers

5 Hedonists (nightclubs, party)

6 Secularists

7 Apathetic (find life painful, ritualise daily life)

Each of these groups receives messages in different ways For example, spiritual searchers are looking for an experience, hands-on stuff, something that will help life to feel more meaningful, whereas corporate achievers want something which tells them how life should be. John Drane suggests that we're probably only reaching the Traditionalists and Corporate Achievers, leaving the other five groups largely untouched by traditional methods of outreach.

In an attempt to understand and reach spiritual seekers, some Christians have begun to take stalls in Mind, Body, Spirit Fairs to talk to people about what Jesus offers. They have offered prayer and ministry of

healing and reported that they had a warm welcome from other stall holders as well as positive conversations with browsers.

Sarah gives her impressions after helping at a Journey Into Wholeness stand at a Nottinghamshire Mind, Body and Spirit Fair.

"As the date for the Mind, Body and Spirit event came close I experienced two different emotions. As I searched out and printed off Bible promises and prayers to make into giveaway cards, and as we met for training and prayer, I experienced a real faith boost. Faith that God was wanting to touch the lives of spiritual searchers and we just needed to be willing to go. The other feeling was fear. Fear that I would let God down; fear that I would be floundering in an alien culture and that I wouldn't be able to love those I met, enough.

My expectation was that although we would probably meet more spiritually hungry people in one weekend than in the rest of our lives, there would be antagonism from the other stall holders and the searchers. I knew we would be entering an alien culture with its own language and I was concerned that in speaking to people we would struggle to find points of contact. Above all I expected there to be bad spiritual 'vibes'.

What I found was acceptance. So many people, stallholders and visitors responded when we 'confessed' to being Christians with 'it's great to see you here – it's about time the churches got involved'. We met lovely, caring people, desperate for something to believe in, who we were able to talk to comfortably about God, our faith, prayer – the sort of things which usually make people look embarrassed and want to change the subject.

It wasn't always easy to work out which of the stalls was offering a therapy that was spiritual in its approach and which were purely physical, but the make up of the stalls was about one third merchandise, one third holistic therapy and one third clairvoyants and witchcraft.

One very sad thing was the number of people we met from a Christian or church background who had been hurt or disappointed by the church and had turned elsewhere to have their spiritual needs met. They needed very little prompting to tell their story and talk about their needs and the problems they faced".

If we know people who are searching in this way, visiting clairvoyants or reading their horoscope regularly, then (rather than be disapproving) we might look upon it as an opportunity to engage them in conversation and to find out what it is they are looking for.

Returning to church, Sarah penned the following words:

'Too often we've been happy to come to Him for blessing
And not been prepared to go out and bless

We've been happy to come to Him for hope
And not been prepared to go out and offer hope

We've been happy to come to Him for comfort
And not been prepared to go out and offer comfort

We've been happy to come to Him for healing
And not been prepared to go out and offer healing,

To a hurting, desperate world, and so the world has looked elsewhere'.

> '**You can make more friends in two months** by becoming interested in other people **than you can in two years by trying to get other people interested in you.**'
>
> **Dale Carnegie**

How willing are we to engage with the spiritual searchers who are almost certainly living and working around us? Do we know how to have meaningful conversations or are we only programmed to give a standard Christian answer?
Can we see opportunities in our everyday encounters?

We need to listen before we speak. We have lots of answers to questions that no one is asking, questions that do not connect with people.
Many evangelism courses consider questions like 'What is God like?' and 'What is sin?'. Yet many people are often not asking those questions. They might be more concerned with issues like, 'How do I live with a diagnosis of cancer?' and 'How can I hold my marriage together?', 'How do I cope with my kids?' and 'How can we survive with redundancy?' As we come alongside people and help them as they ask these questions, we may find that, later, we have the opportunity to answer some of the deeper theological questions, which many evangelistic courses deal with.

A message can be 100% true and 100% irrelevant.

There's nothing wrong with the message we have, and often those around us have not necessarily rejected the message, it's just that it doesn't connect with them because we do not take time to listen to their concerns and questions, affirm them and meet them at their point of need as Jesus did. There is no magic formula for successful evangelism but integrity and common sense are vital ingredients, and we may need to throw stuff out that we've inherited from the past.

The Good Samaritan

So how do we communicate our message with people? Let's begin by looking at how Jesus did it in Luke 10:25-37. The Rich Young Ruler asked Jesus, 'What must I do to inherit eternal life?'

Q How would you answer that question if someone asked you this today?

Q What evidence do we have that many people today are searching spiritually and for eternity?

The Bible is full of direction, guidance and commandments on how to live life in accordance with God's will. In Mark 12 vs28-31 Jesus is asked directly what the greatest, most important commandment is, His answer is one of the most quoted scriptures: "Love the Lord your God with all your heart and with all your soul and with all your mind and with all your strength. The second is this: Love your neighbour as yourself. There is no commandment greater than these."

Your neighbour is not just the person who lives next door to you, or on your street. Your neighbour is everyone who you come into contact with on your life's journey. In Luke 10 vs25-27 there is another account of this command to 'love your neighbour as yourself'. Interestingly, Jesus follows this command with the parable of the Good Samaritan. The parable of the Good Samaritan gives us a very clear picture of loving our neighbour and the responsibilities attached. Q **Read Luke 10 vs25-37**.

Q The man in the story was robbed and left for dead. What have the people round you been robbed of? (e.g. freedom, family, job, health)

Jesus mentioned two different men, both of whom were connected with the work in the temple. All priests were Levites, being selected from the tribe of Levi, but not all Levites were priests. Those who were not priests were assigned duties connected with the tabernacle

> In the time of Jesus, the road from Jerusalem to Jericho was notorious for its danger and difficulty. It was a steep downhill road known as the "Way of Blood" because "of the blood which is often shed there by robbers". It is a distance of 15 miles and would take about 6 hours to walk.

and assisted the priests, prepared the offerings, and cared for the courts and the chambers of the sanctuary.

Q Why might we have expected the priest and the Levite to stop and help? Why do you think they did not?

> Touching a dead body would have defiled a priest or a Levite, which might explain their actions, although they didn't even check whether the fallen man was alive or not.

Often those we need to love and reach out to can be found on our doorsteps and on our own road of life. Notably, the Good Samaritan did not know the person he was helping. The Samaritan 'came where the man was'.

Q Where are people around us today – geographically, emotionally, socially, and psychologically?

> The Samaritans were thought of as pagan half-Jews. They were a sect that grew out of the tribes of Manasseh and Ephraim after their deportation in 722 BC. There was great enmity between Samaritans and Jews at the time of Jesus.

In order to help the man the Samaritan had to get off his donkey.

Q What are some of the 'donkeys' we may need to leave?

Q What did it cost the Samaritan to cross over and help the injured man?

We should not just offer help to those we know well, enjoy helping, or those who have offered us help in the past. It is easy to offer help when it will not cost us time, money or any form of sacrifice. The Samaritan had his journey interrupted, he was not expecting to meet anyone at this moment and the help he gave would have cost him a lot of time. Wherever he might have been going on to, he would have been very late!

Q There are five different types of people in the story, which person do you most relate to?

Music - On the Road to Jericho by Keith Green

Are we now living in

We might not feel particularly at ease in areas which are outside our comfort zone, but that doesn't mean we should avoid them.

Canon John Young says, "Modern Britain resembles ancient Athens – plus mobile phones and parking problems of course. Does this present an opportunity for the Gospel? Clearly it does, but only if modern Christians and the churches to which they belong, are prepared to engage with our secular and superstitious culture with energy, imagination and sensitivity.
Over to you. And over to me."*

In Acts 17 we find the apostle Paul in Athens. Paul wasn't very happy with the mish mash of spirituality that he encountered there but he was able to speak into the culture and use their Altar to the Unknown God to make Jesus known in that place.

Anything could be found on the streets of Athens, and we read that Paul was terrified and angry.
He didn't like what he saw. So, what's new? Paul wasn't at ease with what he saw but he expected to find God there. He was prepared to trust God even on what he felt was dangerous and dodgy territory.

Do we believe that God is at work in the most unlikely places in his world? Some Christians feel that God is doing more outside the church today than he is inside. What do you think? The challenge for us is to ask, what is God doing? Where is he working? How can I get alongside that, rather than insisting that God comes alongside what we're doing.

Paul was alone in Athens, he had no support group. He listened and watched what was going on as he walked the streets and talked to anyone who happened to come along. He got to know some of the intellectuals pretty well through these conversations. Some of them dismissed him with sarcasm, but others listened to him.

Paul affirmed people's starting points. He didn't shake his head in Athens and say, 'we'll need to clear the shelves before we start'. He asked, 'what pegs are there to hang the message on?'. He sees the altar to the unknown God and uses this as a starting point to share the gospel. What are the equivalents in the lives of the people we know?

*John Young, Christian Herald

Ancient Athens?

Bruce's Story

Bruce, the designer of the REJESUS website (www.rejesus.co.uk, a great resource for friends who are considering the Christian faith) gives one example of how this can work.

"This year was my mother's 60th birthday party. She had a big gathering of friends for a weekend of circle dancing, storytelling and music with me there as the son who's into spirituality and stuff. I love rites of passage and ritual and I wanted to create a service to mark the occasion. If there can be dream catchers, animal spirit guides and crystals at the party then I'm not going to leave the real thing outside. So with some minor tweaks to language, I used some fantastic prayers and responses from the Northumbria Celtic Daily Prayer book. I love taking God out to where people are and sidestepping hang-ups about religion that bore me senseless.

One woman who runs new-age retreats told me afterwards that it was a privilege to be there and she only wishes she could have something similar for her birthday. When you taste the real thing you know the difference.

I remember that to most people Jesus is a historical figure not someone who is present. I believe that asking questions is more useful than telling people stuff. I believe that I am nothing extraordinary; I don't feel like I have all the answers and I certainly don't always live life as some shining example of Jesus. Yet at an unconscious level I have come to believe in being real, vulnerable, reflective, genuine and bold - all learned the hard way. And lastly and most importantly I need and like making friends (with or without my faith) and investing in those I already have."

And that is it! Be available and have some fun out there.

Acts 17:16-34

Paul had just arrived in Athens after a successful and eventful visit to Berea. Initially, many enjoyed listening to his new ideas and examined the scriptures with him and became believers. Then other Jews arrived and were threatened by his teaching on Jesus the Messiah and created trouble, Acts 17;10-14. So, as is often the case in his travels, Paul is shipped off quickly and arrives in a new place alone.

He was waiting for his friends and could conceivably have taken a rest or stayed quiet to recover from his Berea experience, but immediately he is aware of the new city and the idols he sees everywhere. Paul had probably never been to Athens before, and like any tourist, he was ready to be very impressed by this incredibly famous and historical city. But when Paul toured the city, he was only depressed by the incredible idolatry he saw all around him.

The idea behind 'given over to idols' is swamped by idols. So Paul saw the beauty of Athens, having the best that Greek sculptors and architects could offer. But all that beauty did not honour God, so it did not impress him at all. He feels distressed about the situation in front of him and sets to work. He sees the spiritual hunger and searching of the Athenians, who sound almost post-modern in their yearning for understanding and acknowledging no single truth. Rather than putting him off, Paul seems to relish the challenge and embrace the intellectual culture of the people he is amongst. **Read vs 16 – 34**.

Q Where are the two places Paul goes to start speaking to people? Why do you think he chose these places?

Q There were four different types of people that Paul engaged with. What do you know about their different points of view?

Q Do you think Paul would have taken time to understand their views and to tailor his conversations to those he was engaged with at that time?

Q What are some of the philosophies of our day? Why is it important that we understand them?

There was sufficient interest aroused by the teaching of Paul for him to be asked to speak at the Areopagus – an important gathering of leaders, a bit like a city council with 30 members out of the city of 10,000, vs 19 & 20. Their question to him was a direct invitation. What an opportunity Paul had created by his initial meetings and conversations!

In verse 21, it talks about the popularity of open discussions about the latest ideas – talking and listening. Paul, whilst he was distressed by all the idols, was excited that here in this city there was an openness to spirituality. Here was a city of spiritual searchers!!

Paul begins his talk positively, he doesn't accuse the Athenians of idolatry or any sin, but acknowledges their interest in the divine. We know that he was distressed by their worship of idols but he didn't display judgement or condemnation, he used terms that would have gathered them in to his speech vs 22 & 23. The word for "religious" used here can have two meanings, either "superstitious" or "devout."

Q What does Paul emphasize as he describes the "unknown god" in verses 24–28? Why might he stress these particular things to this group of listeners?

"They fashioned a tomb for you, holy and high one, Cretans, always liars, evil beasts, idle bellies.

But you are not dead: you live and abide forever,

for in you we live and move and have our being."

Epimenides, "Cretica" translated from the Greek.

Paul uses the altar with the "unknown god" inscription as a "launch pad" to share God's truth.

Q What are the "points of truth" from which you can start to communicate to those in your world?

To draw his listeners in even more, in verse 28, Paul quoted a well-known Greek poet, Epimenides.

Q Why do you think he does this?
Why does Paul not quote the Old Testament in his speech to the Athenians?

Q In verses 29–31, what else does Paul say about God?

Q Why do you think Paul waited to proclaim Christ until the end of his message? How does he introduce the concept of Jesus and what does he emphasize about Jesus?

Q If you had time or opportunity to say just one or two things about Jesus, what would you emphasize?

Q In what three ways did the Athenians respond to Paul's message?

Paul shares the gospel with the Athenians in a way that is relevant, sensitive and uncompromising to the truth.

Q In what ways might you be tempted to water down God's message to groups of people you share with? In what ways are you tempted to be too harsh? How can you avoid either extreme?

Creative Ideas

Take two or three popular songs and look at the ideas beneath them. How would you link a conversation about Jesus to these songs?

Listen to the songs, and write down some helpful notes.

Stairway to Heaven by Led Zeppelin
OR
Imagine by John Lennon
Vertigo by U2
Angels by Robbie Williams
Read All About It by Emile Sande

How Did Jesus Reach His World?

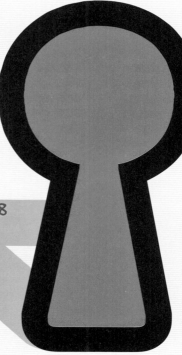

Luke 5:27–31
Work Colleague

Luke 19:1–9
Opportunity/Home

Mark 2:1–11
Home Evangelism

Luke 13:10–17
Sabbath Day

John 5:1–14
Individual

Luke 14:16–23
Banquet

Mark 1:35–45
Village Evangelism

Luke 7:36–50
Dinner Party

Matt 15:29–38
Big Event

Luke 15
Lost and Lonely

John 4:1–42
Social Outcast

Luke 10:25–3
Good Neighbour

Matt 9:1–8
Friendship

Luke 8:1–15
Outdoor

Matt 19:16–30
Topical

John 8:1–11
City Centre

John 3:1–21
Debate

If we look at the many ways and circumstances that Jesus used to reach out to people we might get some clues. Being red hot at Scripture you'll know all these references instantly, of course! This list is an overview of the different types of evangelism Jesus modelled. We can see that there was no set formula – though Jesus didn't sit in the synagogue waiting for people to come in – he got out and about wherever people were, healing and storytelling. We need to follow his example and talk to people about their work, their hobbies, their concerns, and the things that interest them or are pertinent to their lives today. These will ultimately be the pegs on which we most effectively hang our message. We start where people are and gradually find ways to create a forum for further discussion.

Jesus was often to be found eating with people that others shunned. In Mark 14 he's at the house of Simon the Leper, having perfume poured on his feet and wiped with a woman's hair. This was scandalous because respectable women always had their hair fastened up! At other times he's to be found eating with tax collectors. Either way he enjoys relaxing, eating and chatting with people. Jesus often encouraged others to eat in his company. Sharing food together is usually where the best conversations take place.

Clearly, Christians have been able to see the value of relating in this kind of context. Some of the success of the Alpha course is undoubtedly due to the fact that the event is based on a shared meal. When Jamie Oliver produced his little cookery book for Comic Relief he suggested throwing dinner parties to raise money for this charity. The widely-quoted slogan 'Staying in is the new going out' shows that meeting for a meal is an excellent way to relax with friends. And also that there's nothing new under the sun!

If we follow Jesus' example we're likely to be successful in making friends and influencing people, although it won't always be easy. We need to be innovative and creative in re-telling Jesus' stories in ways that listeners can relate to: Jesus talked to the people about vineyards, sheep, farming and fishing, the things that they were actively occupied with. We rather miss the point if we start talking about scattered seeds without explanation in inner city Manchester today.

We also need to not be overly concerned about our reputations. Jesus was often criticized for hanging out with the wrong sort of people. Social outcasts of all varieties were drawn to him. Luke 5 tells the story of Jesus calling Levi, the tax collector, to follow him. Tax collectors were despised in this society. They were excluded from the synagogue; they weren't allowed to be judges or witnesses and their disgrace extended to their family.

Jesus was launching a new style of inclusive ministry here. Is this the attitude we have as Christians? It's interesting to consider what Jesus did with Levi once he'd accepted his call. He didn't take him to the synagogue to begin a nurture group but suggested they went to Levi's house where Jesus could meet his friends, described as 'notorious sinners'.

One of Jesus' most famous encounters is the story of his meeting of the Woman at the Well in John 4. Much has been written about this encounter but it's interesting to note that Jesus actually said very little – he didn't bombard her with information or appear to judge her harshly, but just answered the questions she asked him. How much listening and asking questions do we do, in comparison to how much we talk at people?

Matthew 19: 16-22 is the story of the Rich Young Ruler. What did Jesus talk to him about? Money. And the one above it – debating with Nicodemus, a theologian about theology,'You must be born again'. Nicodemus was a member of the Jewish ruling council who went secretly at the dead of night to Jesus and asked him some questions. He seemed to be sincerely pondering and searching. And because he was a theologian of the time, Jesus presented him with some deep theological thinking. He was meeting Nicodemus 'where he was', speaking to him in appropriately-pitched language, just as he spoke to fishermen about fishing, rich people about money and the woman at the well about water.

Jesus was an expert at picking up the threads of what people were about and working with those. Today, he'd probably talk to people about work, TV (especially soaps), gardening, DIY, fashion and beauty as well as current issues, both personal and national.

Jesus carefully set Nicodemus thinking and gently helped him on his journey; no rush, no shove, no strings attached, no 'in-your-face' pressure for him to make a decision for Christ and sign a form. He let him go away to think it through.

This approach proved effective in

helping Nicodemus grow. In John 7 we see a bolder Nicodemus publicly arguing for fair treatment of Jesus and pointing out the inconsistency of the Pharisees. They were insisting that people kept the law but were trying to sidestep it themselves. So Nicodemus is challenging and insisting on integrity in the midst of this highly irregular proceeding. He makes enough of a stand so that his colleagues challenge him about his allegiance to Jesus' followers.

It is also worth noting what Jesus said later in his initial conversation with Nicodemus. It was to this man that Jesus spoke the famous words of John 3:16, "For God so loved the world..." This is our scriptural gold nugget and it was in Nicodemus that Jesus planted this gold. In the account of Jesus' burial in John 19 we see the spectacular results of this investment: Nicodemus helping Joseph of Arimethea to prepare Jesus' body for burial. It's just hours before the Sabbath, and touching a dead body would have made him ritually unclean for 7 days, requiring purification twice. How would he have explained that away to his peers on the eve of

Passover, a major Jewish festival?

John writes that Nicodemus brought along a mixture of myrrh and aloes, about seventy-five pounds. This was a very large amount, about two large sackfuls. That amount would really only be appropriate in royal burials. It seems as if Nicodemus was making an important statement.

So, although we don't see Nicodemus listed among the names of the believers as the Church grows, he's obviously making progress on his own journey, in his own way; and who knows what impact he was able to make on the lives of other Jews, quietly and studiously?

Did he make use of where God had put him rather than feeling the need to leap into a new life? Maybe. We don't actually need to know. Nor do we need to pin down the people we're sowing seeds with. We can just relax with them, be there for them, try and answer their questions and encourage them. But we don't need to check them for progress unless we're desperate to collect scalps or count heads.

Jesus' Encounters

Jesus' eternity-changing ministry lasted just three years, He was a very busy man with a huge God ordained task. Yet he often showed in the course of his ministry that He was open to interruptions.

Read Mark 5:21-43. A large crowd gathered and was waiting to hear Jesus as he stepped off the boat. Jairus was a ruler within the Synagogue. There were not many men in his position who believed in Jesus at this time. Yet clearly he had great faith in his ability to heal and is quick to ask for his help.

Q How did Jairus approach Jesus and why was this unusual?

Jesus agreed to go with Jairus, and began to follow him to his house. He was on his way to an urgent call that was literally life and death but he was sensitive to the need of a woman who reached out to him.

Q What do you learn about this unnamed woman from these verses? Describe the range of emotions you might be feeling if you were living her life.

She experienced healing instantly and Jesus could have hurried on by, but he delayed his journey further by pausing to find out who had touched him. Her faith is somewhat superstitious. She thinks that if she just touches Jesus' clothes she'll be healed.

Q Why do you think he took time to understand her story and speak to her? What does Jesus do to bring healing to her in ways that far surpass her physical healing?

> **The bleeding the woman experienced would have placed her under the rules of Leviticus 15. She would have been pronounced unclean and would have been an outcast for twelve years. She could not take part in any worship services, nor could she have any public contact without defiling those whom she touched. She might have had to live separately from her husband, and all her financial resources were spent on strange treatments that did not work.**

> **He said to her, "Daughter, your faith has healed you. Go in peace and be freed from your suffering."v 34**

The woman received the health, blessing and the peace that she had sought for so many years. Yet it seemed that this interruption caused a delay that resulted in the death of a little girl.

Q If you were Jairus, what would you be thinking and feeling while Jesus paused and talked with the woman? What thoughts about Jesus might you have had when you heard that your daughter had died? When Jairus learns that his daughter is dead, Jesus encourages Jairus to trust him. What does that kind of trust look like?

Jesus continued on to the house and healed the daughter.

Q What are some of the details that we are given about this story?
   Read vs 38-42. Why do you think these details are included?

The delay resulted in an amazing opportunity to show that he was not only a powerful healer but that his timing was perfect as well! Perhaps when we are too anxious about being late and go rushing past someone who reaches out to us, we should trust in his timing for our lives too!

Jesus invested time in friendships and spent time with people throughout his life and the three years of his ministry. He modelled good friendship when we read of his relationships with Lazarus and his sisters, Martha and Mary.
Read this story in Luke 10:38-42, that comes immediately after the parable of the sower. Picture the scene: a room filled with people listening to the teachings of Jesus. A meal needing to be prepared and only one woman in the kitchen.

Q What do we learn from this passage about the personalities of Mary and Martha?

Which personality type do you tend to relate to more? How would you describe the relationship between Mary and Martha?

Q Which sister was doing the more correct task, according to the culture of the day?

> **Sitting at the feet of Jesus whilst he was teaching was a privileged position, normally all women would have been in the kitchen serving. Jesus was happy that Mary wanted to learn from him.**

Martha asks Jesus - 'Lord don't you care that my sister has left me to do the work by myself?'

Martha knew Jesus so well and had the kind of open relationship with him that meant she felt able to be honest and moan.

Q Are you honest in your relationship with Jesus? Can you tell him how you feel when life feels unfair or a situation seems to be unjust?

Jesus answered kindly, with an understanding that shows he knew and cared for both sisters with their different personalities and needs. He encourages Martha to step away from her tasks and rest and reflect.

Q Do you think we busy ourselves with church activities too often and spend too little time sitting before, adoring and listening to Jesus?

Jesus was able to build the faith of both women through the time he spent with them.

In these different encounters Jesus understands and values each person differently. He never sees people as targets or conquests, he develops friendships, listens to conversations and treats each individual as unique and special.

Q What are the different needs that Jesus responded to in the stories of Jairus, the woman who was ill, Mary and Martha? Did he speak to and treat all of them in the same way?

Master Plan

When a house is being built there is very little to see for weeks because the foundations are being laid.

Psalm 127 says 'unless the Lord builds the house its builders labour in vain'. So Christians acknowledge that everything we do must be wrapped in prayer. We cannot build on shaky ground but only on the rock that is Jesus. So, what guidelines has Jesus given us for evangelism?

In his book 'Prayer Evangelism', Ed Silvoso says that there is only one occasion in the gospels where Jesus spells out an evangelistic method, Luke 10: 5,7,8 and 9.

'When you enter a house, first say, "Peace to this house." When you enter a town and are welcomed eat what is set before you. Heal the sick that are there, and tell them, "The Kingdom of God is near you.'

1. Speak peace to them
2. Spend time with them
3. Take care of their needs
4. Proclaim the good news

This four-step method proved so successful that soon after Jesus taught it to his disciples, multitudes came to believe in Jesus, but unfortunately, these are not the results we see today. What is the problem? Rather than following Jesus' four-step approach we reverse the order and begin with the last step. In most cases, this approach to witnessing does not work.

In the book, Ed talks about our 'circle of influence' and suggests it's important that each of us identify who this group is, in our lives, at any given time. It may be those who live in the homes around ours, those we work with, or the other parents at the school gate. One woman realised that the other women she was receiving chemotherapy with for breast cancer, were her 'circle of influence' at that point in her life.

Take a few minutes to think about who might be in your circle of influence. Consider those who are part of your family, work colleagues, neighbours, and contacts through leisure activities. What are their needs, expectations and interests?

YOU

We will refer to the 'circle of influence' as neighbours here, but adapt that word for those you have now identified as being in your circle.

Sinners loved to hang around Jesus, because there was just something about him that drew others to him. Our neighbours should feel the same way about us, as we are his representatives on earth (Luke 10:16).

Yet, so often we are decidedly unChrist-like in our interaction with those within our circle of influence. We barely put up with them and we make it painfully clear that we can't wait for them to change and become more like us. This is a destructive attitude unworthy of Christ and His kingdom. We must spend time with our neighbours not to patronise or proselytise them but to receive from

'There is nothing I would not do for those who are really my friends. **I have no notion of loving people by halves**, it is not in my nature.'

Jane Austen, Northanger Abbey

them, whether that is with the food, drink or friendship they are offering (Luke 1:7). Jesus' method calls for two-way fellowship with an emphasis on receiving rather than unilaterally giving.

Once you have broken the ice with your neighbours do not rush to share the gospel with them. Spending time is the next step. It provides an opportunity to show unconditional acceptance by welcoming our neighbours just the way they are, instead of the way we want them to be. Jesus instructs us to receive from them. 'Stay in that house, eating and drinking what they give you' (Luke 10:7). When we allow others to do things for us we affirm their value and dignity as God's design and creation.

Blessing opens the door to fellowship and fellowship eventually leads to the third step, an opportunity to meet their felt needs. This will only happen as they trust us enough to disclose those needs. We may then be able to say 'I've been praying for you, let me pray about this too'. Often unbelievers understand prayer better than we do and rarely refuse an offer of being prayed for.

We are not told to bring our neighbours into the kingdom, we are to take the kingdom to them. This is like driving through the desert in an air-conditioned truck stocked with cold drinks. When you spot a weary pedestrian lost on a lonely road on a hot summer day, if you pull up next to him you don't have to beg him to come on board. All you need do is pull over near to him and open the door.

Why should people believe that we, complete strangers, are going to heaven and that they are going to hell? Why should they believe that the Bible is the Word of God? To them it's no different from the Book of Mormon, sayings of Buddha or Mao. What credibility do we have to cause them to believe anything we say? For credibility to develop, a process is necessary and this is where friendship, time, and prayer comes in. Caring for people is at the heart of Jesus' strategy.

So, how much do we care for those within our circle of influence? In his book, Ed Silvoso admits his attitude towards his neighbours needed changing before he could put the principles of Jesus into action where he lived.

"I became aware of my own belligerence towards the lost the first time I tried to implement the Luke 10 strategy in our neighbourhood. Instead of claiming the promises of God to deal with the problems I saw in my neighbours' lives, I told God about everything that was wrong with these people.

I talked to him in disgust about the unmarried mother and how she had to change because she was such a bad example to my daughters. I demanded that he do something about the couple who kept us awake at night with their arguing and fighting. I complained about the depressive neighbour whose garden was a disgrace and brought down the property values in our area. And of course I did not forget about the teenager on drugs. I made it perfectly clear to the Lord what a detriment this young man was to our neighbourhood.

All of a sudden I sensed God saying, "Ed, I am so glad you've not witnessed to any of these yet." Surprised I asked, "Lord, why is that?" His reply was very sobering: "Because I don't want your neighbours to know that you and I are related. I hurt when they hurt. I reach out to them. I constantly extend grace to them. I am the God who causes the sun to rise over the righteous and unrighteous alike. I love them. But you don't. You resent them. Rather than being an advocate for them, a lawyer for the defence, you are instead a witness for the prosecution... if not the prosecutor himself." Then he rebuked me saying,

"Unless you love them, I cannot trust you with their lives."

So there is a need to take seriously this blueprint for evangelism in the gospels. Each of the four points rolls on to the next. When you are friendly to someone you begin to get close. When you spend time with someone you get to know what their needs are. Then you can offer to pray with them. Very few people say no. Once you've prayed for someone the way is open for relaxed conversation. Talk about everyday things that surround you - like Jesus did. Just be yourself - we call it using 'what you've got in the house'. And often you'll get the opportunity (eventually) to talk about your faith in a gentle, non-threatening way that prompts interest and questions.

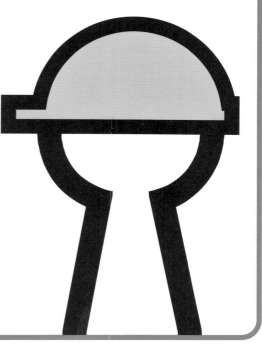

Fearfully and Wonderfully Made

Focusing on evangelism can cause us to see the people around us as 'targets' or statistics. If we are too quick to tell our message before we have taken moments to listen and understand then we are not treating each individual with respect. Let's take time to look at how God sees each person that He has created.

Read Psalm 139

Each one of us is a unique creation of our heavenly Father, the master creator.

A craftsman in medieval times would work for months on a special piece that displayed his finest artistic skill. Finally, when the work was finished, he would present it to the craftsmen's guild in hopes of achieving the rank of master. The work was called his masterpiece. In Psalm 139 we see God, the master craftsman, lovingly at work on his masterpiece. The psalm can have a profound impact on the way we view ourselves and others around us.

> I'll take the hand of those who don't know the way, who can't see where they're going. I'll be a personal guide to them, directing them through unknown country. I'll be right there to show them what roads to take, make sure they don't fall into the ditch. These are the things I'll be doing for them- sticking with them, not leaving them for a minute.
> **Isaiah 42:16**
>
> **The Message**

In God, we are fully known and fully loved which is the theme of Psalm 139. We can only imagine how God impressed these truths on David's heart, but we do know David's reaction to these truths! David was "blown away" by the fact that the all-powerful, all-knowing Designer and Creator of the cosmos was intimately acquainted with him, had personally designed him and cared deeply for him. What significance! What belonging! What value!

The psalm falls into four stanzas. The first three deal with different attributes of this inescapable God as they relate to the individual: He knows everything (vs1-6); He is everywhere (vs7-12); and, He is all-powerful as the sovereign Creator (vs13-18). The final stanza (vs19-24) sets forth the inescapable response to the inescapable God: personal holiness.

Q What specific things does God know about you, from the first five verses?

How does the writer, David feel about God's total knowledge of him? Which of these things is most meaningful to you?

David seems to find this understanding of God's total knowledge of him as overwhelming. His first reaction is to try and hide (vs7-12). He takes an imaginary flight to the furthest places of his imagination and known world, and then realizes that God is there too.

Although we may believe God is everywhere, we don't always experience it.

Q What three sets of extreme opposites does David use to make his point that God is everywhere?

Q In what ways have you sensed God's presence recently? Have you wanted to flee from it? Do you feel near to God or do you feel distant? Is there comfort in knowing that you don't have to "find" God when you need Him? What adjustments might you need to make this week, knowing that God's presence is everywhere?

Read verses 13-16

Q What words are used to describe God's activity and artistry in making us (vs13-16)?

Q According to 139:13-16, when did God first establish a relationship with each of us?

Q What project or activity have you enjoyed doing, planning or making and then, even after your creation was completed, you continued to examine, enjoy, and appreciate it?

> **Like an open book, you watched me grow from conception to birth; all the stages of my life were spread out before you, the days of my life all prepared before I'd even lived one day. Psalm 139:16**
>
> **The Message**

Read verse 16

Q What evidence of God's hand upon your life do you see? How does truly believing that God has ordained your days affect how you make decisions?

Reword verses 23 and 24 into your own words.

In Ephesians chapter 2 verses 4-10 we read that out of all God's creation we are His masterpieces. In the New Living Translation verse 10 reads, 'we are God's masterpiece, created in Christ Jesus'.

Q Do you think of yourself as a masterpiece? Can you see yourself the way God, the master creator, sees you?

Perhaps your group could read Ephesians 2 verses 6 to 10 out loud together.

Q Can we look around and see others as God sees them? If we can see our Father's hand in each person we meet, does it help us to value and treasure each individual?

One of the greatest challenges today is to love our neighbour as ourself.

Sometimes it is hard enough to love those close to us, including our own family. Don Francisco, a popular Christian musician in the 1970s, wrote a song whose words are something we can embrace. 'Love is not a feeling, it's an act of your will'. To love someone is a choice, even those closest to us. Even in marriage, initial romantic feelings of love invariably fade as life, with all its complications and distractions, takes

> **Gen 1:27& 28 Then God said, "Let us make human beings in our image, to be like us… So God created human beings in his own image. In the image of God he created them; male and female he created them. Then God blessed them**

hold. But even when that new romantic, honeymoon period of a marriage cools, we have to choose to love. The same applies with friendships. They won't all be perfect, Instagram-tinted moments, quite simply because none of us is perfect. We all make mistakes, we disappoint others, and we let people down. We choose to love in spite of our fallen human selves. Because love is not a feeling, it's an act of our will.

Q We are all fearfully and wonderfully made. How can we love those who are so different from us or who irritate us? How can we make the choice to love people rather than rely on our feelings?

Love is the greatest commandment. To love others should be our main focus on our journey.

Pray Psalm 139 for a friend or relative who is on your heart today. Do you need reassurance that God cares about those you love? Read and pray Psalm 139, inserting the name of your loved one when you come to the words me, my or I.

Music

Love is Not a feeling – Don Francisco
Psalm 139 - By Sarah Reeves from the album Broken Things
Psalm 139 - Abigail Stauffer from the album Alone to Dream
My Spirit rests in you - Hillsong 1997
I am Amazing - Philippa Hanna from the album Out of The Blue
You Know Me - Stephanie Frizzel, Bethel Music

Creative idea

Bring in copies from Google images of famous masterpieces from the world of fine art- Da Vinci, Michelangelo, Van Gogh, Damien Hirst, Turner. Look together at these amazing works, the pinnacle of a career in art. Bring in some mirrors, and have fun looking at yourself in the mirror – saying, "I am God's masterpiece!".

Difficult DAYS

If evangelism is natural and God-ordained, is it always easy? It is tempting, when encouraging and inspiring others to downplay the potential negatives and just to dwell on the positive success stories.

When a friend asked Claire if she would like to bring her daughter to a special Sunday school event at her local church, Claire said 'yes' straight away. On her first visit there she loved it and felt touched by the Holy Spirit. She came back every week, went off to a Christian camp and couldn't stop singing worship songs. She was on a a fast-track escalator to Christianity.

Many others had been invited to that Sunday school event and had said no. Others friends had been invited to that church and had refused the invitation, or had come once and not returned. Was there a secret formula this time? Just the Holy Spirit at work. The friend who had invited Claire was delighted and amazed that after four years of friendship-building, invitations and prayer, her many attempts at evangelism had finally had one positive response. One yes, after years of 'no, thank yous'.

For most people evangelism is a lifelong calling with only a few precious moments when big steps forward occur. The reality is often stilted conversations, the occasional awkward silence and sometimes rejection of friendship. Some people are not interested, or not ready at that stage in their life and they will reject invitations and not respond to any of your efforts to get connected.

We know that God loves each indivdual as his unique and special creation and longs for everyone to come to him. But he has given everyone freewill and the road to heaven and salvation is a narrow one that not many will take. And when the outcome is a life in all its fullness with Jesus and eternal happiness, then the stakes are high. If we underestimate the task and ignore the opposition we will face then we are likely to go in naively. We should walk in with eyes open and shoulders wide, remembering the words of Paul in Ephesians 6,

10 Be strong in the Lord and in his mighty power. 11 Put on the full armour of God, so that you can take your stand against the devil's schemes. 12 For our struggle is not against flesh and blood, but against the rulers, against the authorities, against the powers of this dark world and against the spiritual forces of evil in the heavenly realms. 13 Therefore put on the full armour of God, so that when the day of evil comes, you may be able to stand your ground, and after you have done everything, to stand. 14 Stand firm then, with the belt of truth buckled around your waist, with the breastplate of righteousness in place, 15 and with your feet fitted with the readiness that comes from the gospel of peace. 16 In addition to all this, take up the shield of faith, with which you can extinguish all the flaming arrows of the evil one. 17 Take the helmet of salvation and the sword of the Spirit, which is the word of God. 18 And pray in the Spirit on all occasions with all kinds of prayers and requests. With this in mind, be alert and always keep on praying for all the Lord's people.

There is a very real opposition, who is fighting to keep the world in darkness and who will do what he can to thwart your efforts.

Rach's Story

We wanted to start a group for young women, to meet up together and have fun opportunities to get to know each other in our community, eventually aiming to weave our faith into natural conversations. We excitedly booked up a big table at a popular Tapas restaurant in our town and eight of us each invited one friend. Four days before we were due to go, the restaurant closed down and didn't think to call us. A friend noticed the sign in their window and called us. We had a frantic evening of calls before we managed to book a Chinese restaurant nearby. For our third event we thought we'd go to a beautiful watermill Arts Centre and hold a fashion show. It was all booked and we had 60 women paid up, when the mill owner heard that we were a Christian group and asked us to go elsewhere as he was a practising witch. We hurriedly booked up the church hall and made the best of it.

During that same year we booked a curry night in a hall on the beach. The curry house turned up 45 minutes late with the food and served it in big plastic buckets – not quite the silver platter buffet experience we had been promised!

When we looked back at all these events, we knew that we were under attack. We tried at all times to have a sense of humour, to work together as a team, and to pray before, during and after every event. Five years on we are still holding events, with a mixture of easy successes, deeper relationships and women coming closer to God, as well as lots of hassle and a few disasters. If we had tried doing it in our own strength or had expected only easy fun and quick success we would have given up long ago!

So it is a reality that some of our friends will reject us and our message. We will get opposition from the devil and events will go wrong. But most surprising is the opposition you might experience from other Christians.

They may not like your style or choice of events or the particular talk that you choose to do or not to do! And they will probably tell you! Quite often those who try out friendship evangelism find that they get more hassle and rejection from other Christian women than from their non-church friends. Perhaps they are jealous of your bravery in trying out new things. Maybe they would prefer you to do other events geared for a wider or different age group or concentrate more on social events for Christians from within the church. We do have to try our best to live in harmony and listen to each other, but we also have to keep our eyes on the task ahead and those who need Jesus. Prayer is key here to make sure your motives are right and to give you wisdom and strength.

So if you face difficult days when trying to build relationships and talk about Jesus, do not be shocked and do not give up. Oppostition may well mean that you are doing the right thing, in the right way at the right time!

"Be strong in the Lord and in his mighty power."

Paul, Ephesians

Women **Collage**

'Don't walk behind me, I may not lead.
Don't walk in front of me, I may not follow.
Just walk beside me and be my friend.'
Albert Camus

Becoming aware of the people around you who don't know Jesus is one thing, getting alongside them may not always be easy or even enjoyable. They may well have very different priorities for you and you may even disapprove of their lifestyle. It's important not to criticise but to try to understand where people are coming from and what has shaped their values and the way they live their lives.

If you read the account of the paragon of virtue in Proverbs 31 you will see a profile of the sort of lifestyle we might all aspire to, someone who juggles successful business transactions, keeps a firm hand on the domestic situation and has the respect of her children, and she also maintains a happy and loving relationship with her husband.

The struggle to juggle those same three situations, work, family and relationships is given as the primary cause of stress for modern women. An Activate supporter, Jill Lawson, has written about how life for many women in the 21st century is far removed from the picture painted in Proverbs:

Ways of communicating with modern woman – who can find?

She is more complex than many microchips.

Her husband lost confidence in himself after his third redundancy,
and the man she lives with now is not her husband.

She brings to this relationship, limited expectations, two children from an earlier marriage
and one born out of wedlock.

Knitting needles she used to employ now act as props for her houseplants
and her sewing machine has gone to the charity shop.

Many clothes she buys from the internet.

She stays up late at night watching recordings of soaps she has missed
while at work during the day.

The family no longer eats together but puts instant snacks into the microwave.

She is not interested in buying a field
but the publicity relating to a Time Share in Lanzarote tempts her.

Her arms are strong as twice a week she pumps iron at the leisure centre.

Her charitable giving is an emotional response to a visual appeal.

She needs tranquilisers to deal with the stress of juggling all the parts of her life.

Her teenagers rarely rise before noon at weekends and,
in spite of all her sacrifices for them, her children call her…
all sorts of names and their bedrooms resemble pigsties.

She laughs rarely, and fears of losing her current man are very real.

She considers suicide, and rape, mugging, cancer and loneliness are a constant fear.

The name of Jesus is often on her lips as a swear word.

This woman really needs to meet him.

But she may not, unless we introduce her.

So let's take a look at some different characteristics and seasons of women today and consider what may well be the underlying causes for their attitudes. Elaine Storkey has given some very real examples of four different women she has come across and touched the lives of.

The Angry Woman

This category of woman is difficult to be with because she's a pain in the neck. Bitter people are draining and time with them needs to be rationed. Sometimes these women are so raw that we feel if the bitterness was taken away there would be nothing left. All we can do is listen to the reasons for the anger and try to address them and support the person.

I knew someone like this and because I listened to her reasons and addressed it, the relationship changed for a while. However, I couldn't maintain a close link, and because her attitude was habitual she found it hard to move on. If you have a fairly constant relationship with an angry person you might be able to find ways to discover what it is that's 'eating them alive', but if you're very close, or if it's your mother for example, then make sure you have some support if you are trying to reach out to an angry woman. Team work and prayer support may be the answer.

The Successful Woman

Following a harrowing session in a radio studio, I went out into the anteroom and started to pray for the presenter, who'd been given a hard time. I suddenly became aware that there was someone else in the room. When I opened my eyes there she was. There had been a break for the news and she'd come out for a cup of coffee.

She asked what I was doing and I said I was praying for her. She said: "Then, don't let me stop you." I continued praying as she sat quietly, and then I hugged her – something I've never done before although I've known her for 15 years. She's not that sort of person. But she said "We women need to stick together. I was so glad you were with me in there." And I was able to share the Gospel with her because she knew I had been listening. I had heard her and understood.

So when you're with the successful woman, look for the stories underneath, because often they will tell of the battles she's had to fight. If she's a particularly strident and objectionable person, it may be because she's had some tough battles and difficulties and somehow that stridency has become attached to her and she's been unable to peel it off. Then you can see if you can help her get back to her vulnerability. Create a safe place where she knows she won't get stabbed in the back or criticised. Go out of your way to get to know her and try to listen and relate.

The Struggling Woman

This is a woman who is finding it hard to cope for all sorts of reasons. She might be OK most of the time, but she's just got too much on and is short of resources or needs to be relieved of some tasks.

She might be just too busy, not competent, she might be lacking in confidence because she's never made her own way, or she might be struggling with something in the past, something she hasn't been able to work through or get beyond and which needs some love and insight.

I know of one woman with a long history of abuse, who is asking, "Where was God? I know he loves me now, I've experienced it now – but where was he in that abuse?". It's a question lots of women are asking, although they might not say it aloud. We need to hear the question, maybe ask it for them.

We need to be honest that we don't know all the answers, and some may need the help of an experienced counsellor. There will be someone you know who has suffered abuse in their background, statistically it's inevitable. For everyone who goes to see a counsellor, there are two people who don't. So many people wear masks. Our task as Christians is not to judge, or worse still to advise them that they must forgive their abuser, but we can just be there to love them and be willing to listen.

The Woman Facing New Things

Women in this category often need help. Sometimes the thing they are facing is a good or positive thing but it brings up things that are not happy. A woman whose baby son died when he was a few hours old, might struggle to respond and adjust when she first gazes upon her newborn grandson.

People facing new things or having old memories re-awakened will quite often need help. We may have to listen in different ways but don't be put off by their apparent anger or defiance. People sometimes need help in making decisions if they are at a crossroads in their life. They may be facing retirement or redundancy, moving jobs, getting married, or deciding about having children. Our role is reaching out, listening where they are and bringing God in.

Don't be afraid of affirming and praising people. Do be afraid of preaching, because they won't hear love, they'll just hear sermonising. They'll think we've got it all together when actually we're all needy people. We're sharing because we're Christians, not because we've got all the answers. We know that God loves us and Jesus died for us, so never be afraid of saying that or of praying for others. Many women are happy to be prayed with, and prayer is easy; it's our lifeblood.

Understanding Women

The four types of women are all real, and probably each of us can think of someone in each category, maybe we can even identify with one ourselves. And depending on what is happening in our lives, all of us have different needs. We wouldn't relate to the struggling woman in the same way as the successful or the angry woman.

These catergories are not new either; women in biblical times can also be looked at in these lights.

Consider the following passages about four women, answer the questions which follow, and ask, 'Who do I know like this?' 'How can I minister to them in their current situation?'

The successful woman: Deborah

Deborah was a judge over Israel, and the only female leader in a culture where women were subordinate. She was trusted, followed God, and led Israel to victory.

Read Judges 4:4-16

1. Put yourself in Deborah's shoes; what would she be feeling in her position?

2. Can you identify any struggles she may be facing?

3. If you were Deborah's friend how could you have supported and encouraged her? What would you learn from her?

The struggling woman: Hagar

Hagar was Abraham's slave woman. Although God spoke to Sarai saying they would have a child, Sarai told Abram to sleep with Hagar to conceive a child.

Read Genesis 16:3-6, 21:8-20

1. Hagar follows Sarai's orders, and then Sarai punishes her and sends her away: what must she be feeling? Have her actions been partly responsible for her situation or is she a victim of circumstance?

2. When in the wilderness, she is at the point of giving up, what are her greatest needs?

3. What did God speak into Hagar's situation?

4. Think of someone you know who is struggling -

   What are their greatest needs? Are they running from anything? How is God telling you to reach out to them?

The Woman Facing New Things: Mary

Mary was the mother of Jesus, a young woman of humble origins chosen to bear the Son of God, to be pregnant before she was married.

Read Luke 1:26-38

1. Mary has just been told by the angel that she will conceive a son; what emotions/questions can you imagine are going through her mind?

2. Her life is turning in a completely new direction, in quite an unbelievable way; what would you say to her if she confided in you? What advice would you give?

3. If you were another person in the village, and heard the news, not knowing about the visit of the angel, how would you react to Mary's new direction? How does knowing 'one more fact', Gabriel's visit, change the way Mary is viewed?

4. Think about people you know who are facing new things. How does Mary's situation and the way she was viewed/treated inform the way we should perceive and come alongside others?

5. Are we able to fully listen, and give people time to talk without jumping in with advice and judgment?

The angry woman: Herodias

Herodias was the sister-in-law of King Herod, who had bitterness against John the Baptist, for he revealed her shame and wrong relationships. She used her daughter to bring about John's death.

Read Matthew 14:1-12

1. Herodias let bitterness and anger at John fester, causing her to take revenge, through her daughter. How do you think Herodias' decision will have affected those around her?

2. Do you think that acting on her resentment will have brought her peace? Why?

3. The Bible teaches a lot about forgiveness (Matthew 6:14-15, Ephesians 4:26). How can these verses help us to relate to women who are experiencing anger and have made bad choices?

4. Who do you know who is battling with anger and resentment?

   What can you offer them to try and bring them peace?

> **Friendship is born at that moment when one person says to another, 'What! You too? I thought I was the only one.'**
>
> C S Lewis

Women's Events - All Too **Girly**?

Sometimes we make the mistake of typecasting women into one mould when we are planning our events.

Not all women like cupcakes, chocolate parties and pink. Some are deeply offended when special female events are laid on and they seem to limit the area of interest to superficial money. Include crafts and food, as well as fashion and image, the environment, sport, outdoor activities, topical discussion, the media... try to think out of the box and wide! But rather than focusing on the ideas that you and your planning committee or church friends will like, think about what your non-church friends will be

Not all women like cupcakes, **chocolate parties and** pink.

topics and image-related subjects. We want to celebrate diversity within our gender and not be limiting or offensive in the way we portray womanhood.

Yet, the reality is that we are never going to please everyone all of the time, and if we did, our choices would probably be so bland and generic that we would only be mildly pleasing and vaguely effective anyway. If you are planning a year of events, then try to think of a range of interests and activities. Build in ideas that are sometimes free, and sometimes cost

interested in. And if you don't know, then ask! And think through the kind of events that they invite you to.

So if they are more likely to enjoy zorbing than flower arranging, even if it terrifies you, go for the zorbing.

What have **YOU** got **in the house?**

The phrase 'What have you got in the house' **reminds us of the story of Elisha and the widow in 2 Kings 4. There was famine in the land and Elisha was approached for help by a widow. The woman was destitute and desperate, and she turned to Elisha for help. His answer turned into a question.**

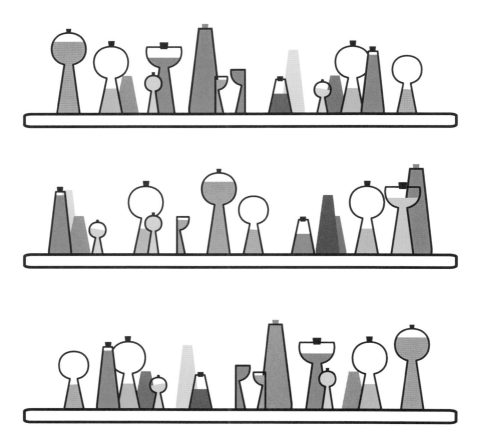

The widow's initial response was that she had nothing in the house at all, but then she told him that she had a little oil. Elisha encouraged her to take what little she had, and step out in faith, and the woman obeyed without question or argument, even though it meant approaching the people around her to ask for jars.

This is a story with a happy ending. God honours her obedience by making the oil flow until she has filled all the jars that she's gathered from the neighbourhood. She was then able to resolve her difficulties, maintain her dignity and bring glory to God. Inspirational! But what can we learn by it?

Well, on a practical level, that God can use a little to make much more. Jesus demonstrated this beautifully by catering for the masses using the contents of a small boy's lunchbox. Hopefully we also learn that, however small and insignificant we consider our talents to be, God can use us in the building of the Kingdom.

What have YOU got in the house? Make a list of the fun things you enjoy. Do you only ever do these activities with other Christians? Could you be more inclusive?

We don't need to bring in experts to do evangelism, or sign up for exhaustive training courses making outreach into a science. We just have to offer ourselves to God and ask him to give us opportunities to take his love into our community. He's made us who we are and planted us where we are.

So don't worry about what gifts and skills you haven't got, just bring 'whatever you've got in the house' to God and be willing to approach the people around you. These can be neighbours, work colleagues, friends, those you meet at the gym, antenatal clinic, or school gate or even in times of crisis, the person in the next hospital bed.

Your circle of influence will be different at various points of life, so always be on the lookout for those who God might want you to include. Always be aware of the things others are interested in and be willing to join in their activities, as well as inviting them to yours. Many people would testify to the fact that it is far more effective to join in with an existing group and be 'salt and light' right there, than to start something of our own.

So let's take a look together around a house and use the metaphors and images connected to each fictional room to inspire you, although of course most of these ideas can be used in any location or venue. Don't always assume that it's right to start one of the ideas in the following pages, but consider where it might be better to join in one that's already up and running.

Come On Over To
My Place

'The Word became flesh and blood and moved into the neighbourhood'.

This version of John 1: 14 from 'The Message' reminds us beautifully of Jesus' role when he lived on earth. Instructed to be 'salt and light' we often find it difficult to know where to begin in building meaningful relationships with those around us. Let's look at a few stories of how some people got started.

'You can't stay in your corner of the forest **waiting for the others to** come to you. You **have to go get them sometimes.'**

A A Milne, Winnie the Pooh

Jenny and Mike's story

If you've lived in your road for many years but had little contact with your neighbours, where do you begin? The Macmillan Biggest Coffee Morning in the World seemed liked a perfect opportunity to get our neighbours together for the first time. Most of them worked so we held it on a Saturday. Although we'd lived in the house for twelve years we were only on nodding terms with most of them, and they didn't know each other either. Macmillan made it easy with ready-printed invitations, which had a space to write the person's name. This meant we had to knock on every door in our road to hand over the invitation personally. Everyone was friendly and told us their name, even if they weren't free to come to the event, which means we've been able to greet each other by name ever since.

An encouraging number came and we had loads of fun as the neighbours all got to know each other that day. As they were leaving someone said 'let us know what you're doing next'. Since then we've done The Samaritan's Purse Shoebox Appeal, a Pamper Evening, a Dinner Party, a Garden Party and watched a film together. Finally we offered an Alpha Course in our home, but only two neighbours came to that. So we need to continue the relationship-building as it seems to be the most effective.

Getting to know people meant that they've shared problems and needs and they've been happy for us to pray with them. Two people have been healed of physical ailments and two other people have become Christians. Our neighbourhood now feels much more like a real community.

One of our neighbours, Mark, wrote the following letter to us, just a year after that first invitation to the Macmillan event.

"I would just like to once again record my thanks to you both for not only becoming close friends, but for helping to drastically change my life. Recently I experienced some sad, low times but, due to your kind and considerate prayers for me being answered by God, I came through those troubled times a much stronger, more experienced person.

By continuing to stick with me you then invited me onto the Alpha course. Midway through this, I experienced new emotions which I believe was God entering my life on a newer, much more personal level than ever before.

By asking me to be a part of your group I have been allowed to develop in a way that years of bodybuilding have failed to do! You have granted me the privilege of having God enter my life because, if you hadn't started inviting me to things, I would have missed out on this totally life-changing experience.

I will never forget your involvement in this process, and pray that we become even closer during the coming year. You both mean a great deal to me and I shall always be grateful for your love.

God bless, Mark xxx
Ps. I am writing this stone cold sober as I have not yet been to the pub!"

But as you'll see from Mark's own account of his story, the pub is one of the places where he can have most influence, in his own inimitable style.

Mark's Story

I started off being a rather ignorant witness because my friends would ask where I was on a Wednesday night instead of being in the local with them. I must admit that in the beginning, I let pride stand in the way of honesty by saying that I had been seeing friends. Once I started to realise that Jesus was becoming an integral part of my life however (about 3 weeks into Alpha), I was honest with them and told them that I was attending a course which was aimed at people like me interested in learning more about the Bible, almost like an idiot's guide to the Bible. I don't wish to sound rude or disrespectful when I use that comparison but having read several of the 'idiot's guide to whatever' books in the local library, I felt that this was a rather useful analogy when talking to my friends in the pub. I believe that Alpha is a very easy to understand introduction that enables the average guy in the street to study the videos, read certain parts of the Bible and think, yes, I understand this, this is what it's all about.

Eventually, it was quite easy being honest to my friends as most are pro-rugby players and are used to playing with colleagues from overseas who have a strong Christian faith so it didn't seem strange for their mate to 'join the gang'. I found it harder talking to the older people I count among my friends. At first they were very sceptical which annoyed me, as they don't seem to have a problem with people in the pub who abuse their bodies on a regular basis. It seemed that they were almost jealous of me because I was participating in something that was against 'the norm'. I saw this as a very sad sign of the times, people taking drugs or getting drunk and no-one seems to bother, yet just because someone wants to find out about Jesus, you get some so-called friends starting to raise their eyebrows!

I have since found that I have had no such trouble either being honest with people asking me about my beliefs or striking up conversations with strangers about what Alpha has done for me as a person. Anyone who knows me will realise what a huge step this is, as I am a very quiet, shy lad. I believe that this inner strength comes from Jesus.

I have since decided to have a tattoo of an image of Jesus that has forever remained in my memory since my attending a local Catholic school in the 70's. Since having had this tattoo done, I have felt empowered in a funny kind of way. It has also provided me with a unique method of witnessing! When I have been in a gym, or at the baths or on holiday complete strangers approach me asking to look closely at the tattoo. This gives them an opportunity to ask about my beliefs, and allows me to explain my feelings and how my faith helps me in life. Indeed, on a recent trip to Spain, which is obviously a very Catholic country I was being stopped every 50 yards (or so it seemed) by locals interested in seeing my tattoo. They all crossed themselves on seeing and touching it, which I found to be a very moving experience. At home, it gives me the chance to discuss religion with people who may otherwise not feel the need to talk about it, maybe in the gym, or have no real inclination to even think about how religion can affect them on a day-to-day basis.

All this has come through joining the Alpha course. Although always religious, Alpha has given me the understanding required to interpret passages in the Bible that I can apply to my life. I am a better person because of this.

Joanna's Story

I became a Christian at the age of sixteen, largely due to the witness of my best friend. None of my family were Christians at the time and my parents' relationship was breaking down. I was finding school very stressful, and a culmination of all this caused me to begin self-harming.

One of the girls in my class, a Christian, picked up on this, although I was not talking to anyone about it and we began to spend a bit more time together. I had already been attending the youth group at our church for a year and seen the influence of the Christian leaders here, who I could tell 'had something special about them.' But it was when I was in my lowest place, when my other friends drifted away because I was quite emotional and not much fun to be around and she decided to be there for me when no one else was, that was when I really saw God's love through her.

I began attending church with her to see what it was all about. That same week I also went to a youth worship event where God spoke to me through a vision he gave to another girl, telling me that He is with me through everything and will get me through anything in my life. I felt His presence that night so strongly, and it was then that I decided to follow Him.

Luke's Story

The first time I was aware of someone having a real faith was when I met a lovely girl called Fi. We were getting on great but she refused my attempts at heading to bed because of her religious convictions. I was firmly agnostic (if that's not too paradoxical). Her stand inevitably made me curious.

After that first meeting we were faced with the reality of a long distance relationship. A three hour commute from Cambridge to York seemed rather ridiculous to me and for Fi, a poor student, travelling by train regularly would be impossible. So when we reached the point where reality struck and it seemed like there was no future for us, Fi (with the help of wine) booked a train ticket for Cambridge. In the morning she tried to cancel it only to find it non-refundable. So she came to Cambridge and we both, rather nervously, embarked on our first real date. To our relief we found the awkwardness disappeared and we knew we wanted to make it work.

After maybe a month or so of myself commuting to York every weekend, she asked me to go to church with her. Out of mild interest, but mostly to keep her happy I agreed. The service itself was as dry as the Sahara, and the only thing I found of interest in that building, apart from Fi, was a homeless man dressed in rags who seemed to take comfort from the priest's words. Afterwards we had a conversation about the evening, but nothing of importance was said except for her comparison and reflections on her home church.

Some time later I had the challenge of meeting the parents. This went well, except for her father's desire to torture me by pretending to take offence at the word "bloody"; it has since left my vocabulary. That Sunday I visited their home church and had a very different experience of church. The worship was lively, the preaching energetic and the people very friendly. It was the people most of all who made the experience so memorable. Despite being asked several times when I was planning to pop the question (at the time we had only been together six months), I found the people were so welcoming and there was a true sense of family, something I really desired.

When my birthday came around, to my surprise Fi's parents gave me my first Bible. At the time I would have rather had the money but this Bible would be used to change my life. After visiting their church a few more times I became curious why so much time was afforded to this book. Curiosity got the better of me and I started to read it and I was taken aback. The words I mocked in my youth became truth to my eyes, I couldn't put it down. I felt this was the truth I'd been searching for, the God who saved me wrote these pages for me to read. I started in Genesis powered on through Leviticus and Numbers and before

I knew it I was at the Gospels.

Fi and her family became invaluable to me here as, although I was reading and understanding a lot, I wasn't quite sure what to do with some of the more difficult passages. From them I received many answers but was encouraged to ask God for others. This taught me to pray. Finally I gave my life to Jesus 24th December 2009 and was baptised shortly after. Fi was with me every step of the way and as I drew nearer to God she too drew closer with me and we had some great conversations along the way. When we finally got married on the 14th August 2010, I'm so glad that we entered into our vows knowing Jesus.

In this we were able to start our marriage on the true foundation, in contrast to the start of our relationship. Although I regret many of our actions before marriage, I don't regret having been on that journey together as we are certainly the stronger for it for which I am eternally grateful. I am now studying theology at college, enjoying delving deeper into my faith and the Bible.

Matt's Story

Matt was a student, studying for a degree and working in a pizza restaurant to supplement his student loan. One of his fellow waiters, Dave was in his thirties, and well travelled. His usual pattern was to stay in a place for six months or so and then move on, sometimes to another town, often to another country.

Matt and Dave often had interesting talks when business was slack and they shared a love of some very different types of music. Dave was a Johnny Cash fan, and he often pondered the meaning of the lyrics in his songs. One evening, while listening to 'The Mercy Seat' he was struck by the words and wanted to know more about what the mercy seat really was. The following evening as they served pizza together, Dave asked Matt what he knew.

Later that week Matt found himself at Dave's flat, Bible open, looking at all the Old Testament references to the mercy seat. Much discussion followed and although Dave has now moved on, the conversations he and Matt had, often based around Johnny Cash's songs, will be long remembered, and eternity may show that these were the beginning of something more.

Let's not make the mistake of having a secular and sacred divide in our lives. Let's remember that wherever we go, God has been there before us. He's working in the lives of those around us, in ways we may have no understanding of, but we need to be open to him and others and come alongside what he's doing.

The Front Door

As we tour the house and discover a host of different ideas, don't let the size or number of different rooms distract you from the possibilities in your home. None of us has all of these rooms! Have an open, positive mind that will let our ideas inspire you to think through what will work for you, in your home, in your community, with your friends and contacts. Some of us live in comparative luxury while others of us struggle to make ends meet. But, whether you're a student trying to squash just one more person into your already heaving study bedroom or have plenty of space, ask God to show you the possibilities as we go around the rooms of this imaginary house. The Holy Spirit is standing by to nudge you with ideas just right for you...

In Hebrews 13:3 we are commanded, 'Do not forget to entertain strangers, for in doing so, some have entertained angels without knowing it', but how welcoming are you? Do you have a heart to reach out to others? Does your front door portray this? If your door has no knocker, a bell that doesn't work and stickers announcing – "Beware of the Rottweiler, CCTV – You are being watched, No Callers without prior appointment, Keep Out" then your neighbours might think twice before calling to see you for a friendly chat.

Some of the grander new developments that are being built offer high security such as walls, automatic gates. With internet connections and shopping, people need never venture into the outside world. This level of security would be very effective at keeping intruders out, but surely runs the risk of making the residents feel isolated and imprisoned.

So we need to keep a sense of proportion about safety issues. And, even if we can't literally leave our doors open, we can have an 'open door' mentality and be willing to open our homes and hearts to people. It's not always going to be easy and, inevitably, you'll enjoy the company of some people more than others. But as a general principle, have an open door in your home and your heart.

The Hall

'It's the friends you can call up at 4am that matter.'
Marlene Dietrich

The telephone table

It's good to talk – and your telephone can be a means of bringing God's love into other people's lives. Those who are housebound or have long-term illness can often feel forgotten and a cheery phone call can be a great tonic. Mobile phones have been around for 40 years now and their use is so widespread that some have started to believe that home phones will disappear, but 85% of homes in the UK still have a landline. So pick up the phone and call someone in the tradtional way; they will appreciate your effort and the lack of distractions. This might be particularly true of the older generation. Someone who might be embarrassed by prayer face-to-face will often be really blessed if you pray for them over the phone. Even if you can't get out much yourself you'll be able to do this. So do think about ringing someone who is lonely and bring a bit of God's love into their day.

Research shows that we check our mobile phones, on average, every six and a half minutes. So keeping in touch with your circle of influence is easier than it has ever been. People like to stay connected and sometimes relationships are about finding the right way of communicating at the right time. Texting a short message reminds people that you are thinking about them without interrupting a busy moment. They have a choice about when to respond and can take their time thinking through their reply.

Invitations to events can be done quickly, yet personally through a group text. It is easier to be brave with a text invite than face to face! The fear of rejection is lessened as people are more comfortable checking their own diary and getting back to you when they know their schedule.

It is good to be senisitve and use different methods of communication to match each friend. Some prefer a quick regular text, others like to find a message on their mobile and call you back later. Others may find speaking difficult and have become more confident socially with the arrival of email, typing their thoughts and checking them before pressing send. And there will always be some friends who prefer the home landline long chat.

Being a good friend today is all about finding and adapting your style of keeping in touch. If your friend writes you a long handwritten letter on Basildon Bond embossed paper and pours out their heart and wishes, then a quick reply by text is not going to be appreciated! Be prepared to be sensitive to others' wishes and match your comminication styles, as well as looking out for how technology changes and adapting. It may be FaceTime and WhatsApp today and something new tomorrow.

Your list of phone contacts

A well-known sales strategy is that nearly everyone knows a circle of people, who know a circle of people, who know a circle of people. Through one very positive contact you could reach as many as 250 by word-of-mouth recommendations.

If we experienced really good food and service at a new restaurant, or found a fantastic bargain, we probably won't be shy about sharing and our whole network will quickly know about it, but what about the good news of the gospel? How many of our friends, neighbours and colleagues do we want to see come to a living faith in Jesus? Eternal life is a free gift to all, but we tend to feel it costs us our reputation to tell others.

As you start to build relationships with others they will begin to be real with you. Hopefully, they will see something different or special about you that will prompt them to ask questions and give you the opportunity to share something of your life with them. You may never need to try to artificially engineer the conversation, but simply be ready to answer their questions.

As 1 Peter 3:15 says, 'Always be prepared to give an answer to everyone who asks you to give the reason for the hope that you have. And do this with gentleness and respect.'

Hats & Coats & Gloves & Scarves & Boots

You won't always want to stay in with friends. The hall is where you hang everything you need to step out into the great outdoors. Walking has been proven to be the best exercise ever. It trims your hips and thighs, strengthens your lungs and heart, and sparkles up dull hair, skin and eyes. If you're a fair-weather walker, remember that exercising in cold air burns off more calories than in summertime. It is also a great opportunity to talk.

Many of Jesus' discussions took place on the move. People are often much more relaxed about asking questions and discussing things when you are walking side by side, as opposed to sitting face to face.

So why not rally some ramblers, or lead a dog walk? It's much safer walking together than alone and can be great fun. Maybe the group could take turns at finding new routes and organising trips further afield.

The AA book 'No Through Road' contains lots of circular walks but look out in the local press and bookshops for others near you.

Stand at the crossroads and look; ask for the ancient paths, ask where the good way is and walk in it, and you will find rest for your souls.

Jeremiah 6:16

The Lounge

Film Club

Films are a great way of sparking thoughts and discussion. So why not join a group in your area or start your own film group? You could begin by inviting everyone to bring a short film clip (max 5 minutes) which they feel outlines their world view. They can give a short verbal introduction to explain what they are going to show, which must not be longer than their clip.

After this you can agree on the next film – ask everyone to watch it in advance and show clips to discuss; or you can continue to bring clips from films or soap operas and share thoughts. Some have been put off the idea of a film-watching club as it seems too long an evening to gather, chat and then watch a two hour film before refreshments, leaving no time for discussion. So the key, unless you have enough spare time for very long evenings, is to plan, watch and prepare clips in advance. Log on to the Damaris website, www.damaris.org for details of a range of contemporary films and discussion questions. Favourite discussion starters are **'The Matrix'**, **'The Truman Show'**, **'Les Miserables'** and **'The Life of Pi'**.

If you feel your guests are ready for a slightly more up-front message, then why not lend them a Christian film?

'Tales from the Madhouse' contains 8 x 14-minute atmospheric and arresting monologues by people who had contact with Jesus: People like The Thief on the Cross, The Centurion, the wife of Pontius Pilate and Judas, the Betrayer.

'3 Days that Changed the World' tells the Easter story with a sharp, contemporary edge. Following the thoughts and memories of Rob, a character reflecting on the meaning of Easter, the viewer is drawn into thinking about Easter and challenged to discover more.

'The Passion' was a major box office success which generated lots of discussion. It may be more appropriate to lend this video out and then discuss it informally at a later date.

'The Bible: The Epic Mini series' has been very popular and is divided into short episodes.

All of these dvds may be available through your local Christian bookshop or Amazon UK.

Discussion groups

Steve and Jane hold a Talkback group in their home every fortnight. Everyone brings something to the group that has made them feel 'Mad, Sad, Bad or Glad' since they last met. This might be a newspaper cutting, a poem or extract from a book, a piece of music or film clip, a photo, a personal situation – or even a box of treasured memories.

Talkback groups give the opportunity for lively discussion, followed by drinks and refreshments, and there's rarely enough time to cover everything that the participants want to say. The issues of life and death are always on the agenda and the Christians in the group often have an opportunity to share something of their faith or on occasions to pray for others.

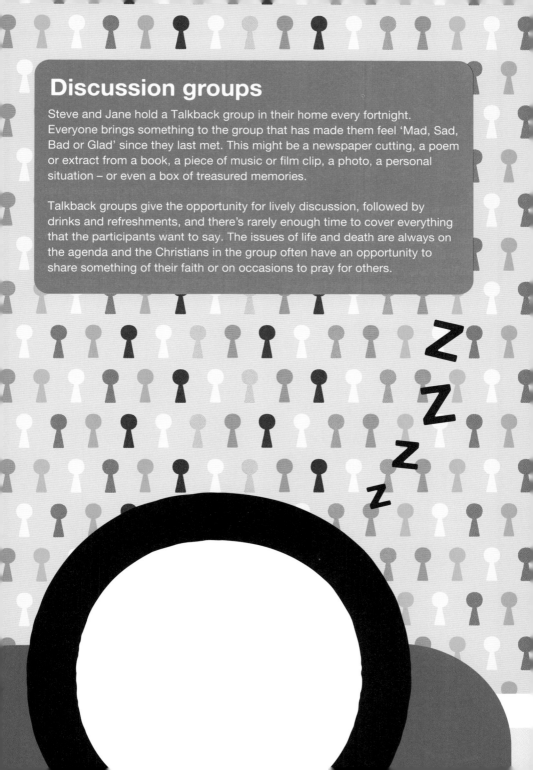

Achkiy Parties

The word 'Achkiy' is a native Peruvian word meaning 'anything that shines', reflecting how the Achkiy project (started in 1996 by Julia Crellin, Fiona Castle's daughter) is bringing light and hope to the lives of many. Julia has encouraged and taught women from a shanty-town near Lima, Peru to make jewellery using gemstones and top quality silver. They also use recycled paper to make attractive hand-made cards, notebooks and bookmarks, which they sell at about half the price of similar products in British commercial card shops.

Anyone can consider having an Achkiy party in their home as a way of getting to know their neighbours and sending much needed funds to this project. It costs nothing to have an Achkiy party. Invitations, a selection of products on a sale or return basis and a 12-minute video demonstrating the work are supplied, so you don't even have to try to explain it to your friends. The response has been overwhelmingly positive; lots of people from schoolchildren to grannies have held parties in homes, workplaces and school fairs, which has made a huge impact in Peru, but also is helping to break the ice in neighbourhoods all around the country. www.achkiy.com

Television

In a recent lifestyle survey 99% of both men and women said that their favourite relaxation was watching TV. Some programmes require very little of us other than to sit passively and watch – though soaps are a great source of discussion and if you see something worth recording you can catch the omnibus edition later.

Sports programmes are good communal watching, especially for men – so why not invest in a large screen television and guarantee that your house will be a favoured venue for sports events like football and Wimbledon? Offering pizza and beer will improve the stakes significantly – food is always a great way to relax and stimulate discussion.

You could easily extend this to include quiz shows and debates. Occasionally television series really capture the imagination of the public. 'Dowtown Abbey' has been a big hit, and gathering friends around, dressed up in period clothes to eat themed snacks and watch the next episode together might be very popular.

Series-long competitions bring opportunites to invite a group round to watch a final together, whether it is 'The X Factor', Britain's Got Talent' or 'Strictly Come Dancing'. These programmes stretch across the generations and from auditions to weekly rounds, build up to the finals. Voting within the room can bring added excitement.

As Christians we can use all types of media for good. Often our voices are only heard in complaint when something offensive galvanises us into action. And actually contacting the right authorities is effective. Every time OfCom receives even one complaint, it investigates; it only takes ten complaints for OfCom to register the issue on its website weekly bulletins. We can make a difference! And it is important to remember that positive comments are just as effective and important when it comes to future budget and programming decisions.

Useful email addresses – try to use them more to congratulate than to complain:

Television
consumers.ofcom.org.uk

Adverts
www.asa.org.uk

Film classification
feedback@bbfc.co.uk

Well Women Workshops

Well Women Workshops are a series of sessions designed to encourage women coming out of depression, bereavement, abusive situations, mental illness, or merely feeling 'stuck in a rut', to begin to feel ready to face the big wide world again.

The aim of the workshops is for women to grow in self-awareness, confidence and self-esteem, and to begin to see life from other perspectives. Women are encouraged to be more 'others centred', to focus on giving and hospitality, and to make lasting friendships with others who may be like-minded.

The workshops are a course of 8 sessions held in a home setting, where a group of 6 – 10 women meet together to discuss issues such as physical, emotional and spiritual well-being, as well as issues around home versus employment and creativity and social awareness. Referrals come informally by personal recommendation, and by just chatting with people and formally from health centres, social services and other voluntary organisations providing services for women. Rarely a day goes by without the organisers receiving a phone call from one agency or other enquiring about what Well Women Workshops do.

Three Christian women run the workshops but they are keen not to 'push' Christianity on those who attend the group but prefer to speak of their experience of God through their own personal testimonies.

Many women feel isolated within their homes. They may be new mothers, their children may have just started full time school, they may have retired early due to ill health or they may have recently retired because of their age. Feelings of isolation can lead to depression, and a sense that their situation is beyond repair, that life is awful and there is no way out. There's a saying that 'a problem shared is a problem halved' and Well Women Workshops find that women enjoy going into a home environment to chat, drink coffee and eat cake! The three trainers speak about their own personal struggles with great honesty and this helps the women to open up about their struggles, to see that they are not isolated with their problems, that there are other like-minded people with similar, or even worse situations, and what's more, there is a way out. They speak about deep issues and they cry. They also have lots of fun, and have a good laugh, too. Finding a balance is essential for everyone's sanity!

One woman who attended a recent workshop said her self-esteem was 'like a slug's belly on a paving stone'. She felt she had nothing to offer people, and was terrified of any form of hospitality. She now hosts a home group, has accompanied a blind gentleman to a conference to help him around, attends several other groups, and recently provided a rather delicious pudding for a Well Women lunch.

Another woman was recently bereaved, having cared for her mother for a year. She is a young Muslim mum who Jill, one of the organisers, met in the school playground. She had to force herself out of her house in order to take her son to school. Jill noticed that she looked rather 'lost' and befriended her, and gently persuaded her that the workshops might be just what

she needed. She reluctantly agreed and gleaned so much from the group. By the end of the course she was perfectly comfortable leading exercises from the flipchart. She looked good. She had her hair done. She went on to do voluntary work in the school, and is now doing a counselling course, and is a different woman who is now looking out for people herself in order to befriend them.

If you are interested in running a series of Well Women Workshops in your local area contact Jill on abrahart@btinternet.com

The Kitchen

However high or low you might rank in celebrity cook status, there is no doubt that the kitchen is the heart of the home, and there is something about the casual intimacy of this inner sanctum that invites shared confidences. Tea and sympathy are a heady mix over the warm security of the kitchen table. Transport the action into the relative formality of the lounge and the atmosphere is completely different.

Cookery

So why not make a date for a regular one-to-one in your kitchen with a friend? If you feel guilty just sitting or haven't really got the time you could plan to do your ironing or cook together as you chat and use the time productively. Some Christians have given time and cookery skills to lead a small class – either in their own homes or in the local community centre at a family support group. They give advice on nutrition or cookery on a budget and demonstrate easy recipes. It's good fun, a way of sharing your gifts and everyone gets to take something home for tea.

Breadmaking

One Methodist minister in Liverpool has set up bread-making sessions as an alternative way of doing church. When the bread is in the oven everyone gathers to consider a Bible passage. Participants are invited to offer prayers for themselves or others and light one of a collection of candles in a large dish on the table. Afterwards some of the bread is eaten at a community meal, and local churches distribute the rest.

Why not try gathering a group to make bread? Kneading the dough is a great way to get rid of anger and frustration and the space created whilst waiting for the dough to rise and the bread to bake can become a discussion group session. Afterwards you can share the bread with cheese, salad and some soup.

Chocolate Parties

Judy organised a Chocolate Party at a local hotel, but this idea works just as well in a home.

"The bar was open as people arrived for a complimentary drink included in the ticket price and we began with a few facts about chocolate, comparative calories, why it is good for you and giving 'permission' for everyone to be off diet!

- We showed two short video clips (about 3 minutes) from the film 'Chocolat' and there was an opportunity to discuss the issues raised

- This was followed by a video demonstration by Delia Smith, Truffle Torte from her Winter Collection. We didn't have the facilities for an actual demonstration but the video worked well

- We had a number of tables set up around the outside of the room with tried and tested recipes for tasting - everything in small portions, plastic plates and teaspoons -lots of things to try, including the Truffle Torte

- Chocolate fondues – we managed to gather 10 chocolate fondue sets with tea lights underneath to keep the chocolate melted. With each

'There is **nothing better than a friend,** unless it is a friend with chocolate.'

Linda Grayson

fondue was a platter of fresh fruit pieces – visual effect quite stunning

- We used and displayed Fair Trade chocolate and other goods and information

- There were also other fun things – guess the number of Smarties in the jar. Predict which kind of Revel you are eating. Two Quiz sheets to complete and an information sheet to read through

- We had stations for tea, coffee and hot chocolate. People then took their drink and sat down and marked the quizzes – answers up on PowerPoint saved time. Prizes were given. It was a great success".

Cake Club

The latest new excuse for gathering, and enjoying delicious food, is a cake club. Each friend brings a cake large enough to be cut into at least eight slices, a table is set out to display them all, then mass tasting occurs before recipes are exchanged. Some clubs swap the remainders of each cake so that the guests take home a mixture of flavours and textures. Friends of mine wax lyrical about lemon drizzle, victoria sponges and chocolate gateaux but cupcakes and brownies are banned! They call themselves 'cakies'.

There is also a network called 'The Clandestine Cake Club' which takes the simple cake meeting formula and adds secret locations with only an email link. The internet blurb says – 'Arrive as strangers, leave as friends. It's all about Cake!' So if you have moved to a new area and want to meet other cake lovers then try
www.clandestinecakeclub.co.uk

'Cake is happiness! **If you know the way of the cake, you know the way of happiness! If you have a cake in front of you, you should not look any further for joy.**'
C JoyBell C

Healthy Eating

We're all now very conscious of what we eat and 'Healthy Eating' is a great platform for a variety of events, from discussing one of the many 'foodie' books to swapping ideas for kids' lunch boxes. There is perhaps no other time in the last decade or so when healthy eating has been so prominent on the agenda for a lot of people. It seems that from every angle, media, friends and medical experts we are being encouraged to strip the fat down and up the healthier option.

Curry Evening

This is a great, fun and econmical way of bringing people together. Invite your friends and ask them to bring or prepare their favourite Indian dish; hopefully there will be a mix of chicken, beef and pork as well as vegetarian dishes.
If possible try to have a range of curry strength too, with mild Kormas for the nervous palate through to Vindaloo for the brave.You could provide the rice and nan breads and mango chutney. The feast will be a shared experience with all the dishes in the centre and everyone sharing.

An eaiser alternative, and a great spontaneous winner, is to buy it all in from an Indian take-away and just text your friends, mentioning a curry get together for £5. Add to the experience by opening the containers in the middle of the table and not telling everyone the names of each dish. This encourages a good guessing game as well as inspiring folk to try new tastes. Many consider curry to be the new national British dish!

Fruto del Espiritu

Fairly traded fruit cocktails! A group in Thame organised a Fruto del Espirito event on a cold January evening. The hot-spiced tasters, 'calientes' were very welcome, and it was fun, as well as providing a good talking point, as the guests wandered about chatting and looking at the posters and literature on display. Rutie, who set up the project, gave an excellent and inspiring talk about the fruits of Colombia and her hopes and aspirations for the business. Everyone who came agreed that it had been a really great way to entertain friends – a bit like a fun cocktail party. What is more, they were inspired to spend generously, because they really liked the products.

A Fruto del Espirito event combines supporting a fair trade project in Colombia with a fun evening tasting and drinking a variety of fruit purees. It includes a demonstration of how the fruits can be used to make exciting desserts and drinks which provide a good talking point as awareness is raised of the plight of two million displaced people in Colombia. They have lost homes, farms, livelihoods and family as a result of the extreme violence which has engulfed the country, often financed by the drug trade. Investment in the fruit industry contributes to peace, offering a future and a hope to small farmers and displaced people. Fruto del Espiritu was created to open up new overseas markets for exotic fruits, developing new products and ploughing profits back into the fruit sector. If you are interested in buying the products or running one of these events contact Rutie at info@fruto.co.uk for more information.

Meals that serve

Pete and Gina's Story

Another creative way to incorporate food into connecting to others is to take it outside the kitchen and dining room and to the home of another by means of service.

"When my children were starting school I met Tracey, a young woman whose daughter was the same age as my eldest and we connected almost immediately. Over many months our daughters enjoyed days out and sleep-overs and Tracey would often find herself at my house chatting in my kitchen or round my table enjoying lunch. Not long into our friendship, however, tragedy struck as Tracey was diagnosed with cancer. For the best part of ten years Tracey fought her cancer, enjoying the reprieve of long periods of remission only to be plunged back into despair as the cancer would return.

Eighteen months ago her cancer returned once again and this time with merciless force. Tracey began finding even the smallest of things very demanding and exhausting. Feeling deeply moved by her situation, I made the commitment to her that I would bring her at least three meals every week for as long as she needed. She insisted that was too much to expect, after all, I did have four children and a husband to look after, she didn't want to be a burden.

Nevertheless, my husband and I committed to cooking and delivering several meals every week and did so until she was ultimately admitted into our local St Catherine's Hospice. The prognosis wasn't good: for the first time in a decade Tracey's time on this earth was being counted out in days, as opposed to months and years. My husband and I continued to provide meals for her husband while he desperately tried to spend every waking hour by her side. On our visits to the hospice Tracey, who as yet had not made any form of conscious acknowledgement of faith, thanked us repeatedly for our kindness in providing the meals for all those weeks and continuing to do so for John, her husband.

She then, quite surprisingly, asked my husband if he would take her funeral. Talking to her about what she wanted at her service, was perhaps one of the most difficult things my husband had had to do in his role as a pastor. During those moments, sitting at her bedside, walking through what Tracey wanted in her service, my husband had the opportunity to talk to Tracey and John about God, life, eternity and death. It was a moment of privilege that, we are convinced, would never have come our way had we not served her and her husband in very simple and practical ways".

'Strange to see how a good dinner and feasting reconciles everyone'
The Diary of Samuel Pepys

Rhiannon's Story

When I joined my local Slimmers' World group I quickly made friends and got into conversations around how to eat healthier without losing the enjoyment food brings. Some of them ended up coming along to my open-house lunches with a distinctly healthy theme. Food would be cooked in accordance with the various slimming book recipe suggestions. Other times we'd simply enjoy what we called our little "Lunch Pot" times. Top of the menu would be Slimmers' World cottage pie.

After a while we took it in turns to cook different dishes, and the get-togethers would centre around enjoying healthier food and swapping recipe ideas, whilst encouraging one another to stick with the diets and lose the required weight. A few pounds were shed as the friendships grew!

Fair Trade

Contact Traidcraft on www.oxfam.org.uk/fair for a selection of fairly traded chocolate and food. Fair Trade events are always popular. Logging on to a site like www.fairtrade.org.uk will give up to the minute information on events nationwide and ideas on how to get involved. Fair Trade fortnight is usually held at the beginning of March each year.

Sharing Food

In a recent Social Survey, people were asked to list their favourite leisure activities. Watching television came out on top across the board (99%) but a close second, 97% for women and 95% for men was having a meal with friends.

Food is a common denominator - we all have to eat. This can be a perfunctory exercise, absentmindedly eating a sandwich while opening the post or watching TV, or it can be made into a pleasurable social occasion by sitting around with friends. You don't have to go overboard with the catering, unless you really enjoy cooking. Just serve simple food so that you can relax and enjoy the evening. You can even share the catering and let others bring the pudding. People tend to come for the company not the food. If cooking isn't your thing buy a 'take-away' or 'ready meal' and 'assemble' it yourself. You can use traditional events as excuses for a grand meal, like Thanksgiving and Christmas, and choose your menu accordingly.

Let others share in the preparation or the washing up if they volunteer – you can have great conversations while peeling carrots or wiping dishes. The aim is to get to know people, not to exhaust yourself trying to be a faultless hostess, which can intimidate others. You could invite neighbours from other cultures to bring samples of their traditional dishes.

The **Dining Room**

Bring Your Roast Dinner

Everyone loves a roast! But sometimes the work and the cost involved in preparing all the side dishes would put you off inviting others round. So, share it out! Ask everyone to play their part by bringing a chair, a plate and the relevant cutlery. Ask them which part of the traditional roast accompanimnets they like to cook and invite them to bring that.

Offer to cook the actual meat roast, warm the plates then sit back and watch as the meal comes together.

If the weather is right, go for an outside table and see how delightful it is to watch an old-fashioned eccentric garden party come together. Some might bring napkins, all the dishes and plates will look different. One friend went all out, and arrived with a vintage table cloth and an old silver candelabra!

Everyone will feel very spoiled and leave declaring it the best dinner ever, and all for relatively little cost and effort on each individual. Entertaining is sometimes at its best when it is a shared venture, without all the stress, attention and glory going to the host.

Thanksgiving Dinner

Guy was leading a project with three others some years ago. They were travelling the country and working long hours at the office to meet deadlines, so his wife, Caroline, suggested he got the team together with their partners for dinner to give everyone a chance to get to know each other socially.

They all got along really well and after that first evening, another person offered to cook a meal a couple of months later. They were never legalistic about it as they agreed that social ping-pong could be a pain if you don't feel like joining in, but everyone felt that it was a good idea to meet regularly. Even though the project finished years ago, they have continued to meet as friends.

The other three couples were not Christians and one husband was fairly 'anti' at first, though he was never unfriendly. However, he gradually began to thaw and chat easily with Guy and Caroline about their faith. His wife became a Christian recently and they all went to the service when she was confirmed in their local Anglican church. They've now all been to church together occasionally on special occasions.

This year Guy and Caroline decided to invite the rest of the group for a meal in November and suggested a dinner at Thanksgiving. They were all asked to come with something in mind that they were thankful for in their lives and they all seemed very comfortable with this idea.

They just chatted as usual over the meal, and the things that everyone was grateful for came out very naturally. The topics included health, relationships, children and leisure so there was no strain or embarrassment involved. At the end of the meal Caroline just said she wanted to say a brief prayer and thanked God for their lives and all the things they appreciated and enjoyed.

There wasn't any blinding flash of lightning for anyone but it was a good opportunity for people to express gratitude and for them to see Caroline pass those thoughts to God in a relaxed chatty way, rather than the formal churchy manner they possibly expected.

This kind of stuff is seed sowing. The group accept Guy and Caroline because they are fond of them as friends and through that association, God comes into focus occasionally and naturally. On one occasion, Caroline rang one of the wives because she was on her mind. It was a timely call because she was very low about something and her husband later commented that he found it amazing that Caroline had been prompted to ring her just at that moment. God is in with a good chance with this gang!

Dave's Story

Dave met Andy through a colleague at work and over the course of a few weeks they had some conversations about the Christian faith. One day, Andy told Dave he'd been talking to some of his other friends about their conversations and invited Dave to a supper party he was planning, so he could tell these friends what he believed.

Dave discovered that a very diverse group of guests had been invited. There were two neo-pagans, into tarot cards and conspiracy theories, an ex-Hindu, two were arty types, and a seriously ill ex-serviceman partnered by a business consultant thirty years his junior. In addition, there was a bell-ringing author who didn't like people disagreeing with him, and an aetheist from the legal profession who was heavily into politics. Dave was given five minutes to explain what Christianity is about and then it was over to the other guests for questions and chat.

The conversation which followed covered other religions, suffering, how can you know God exists, surely as long as you're spiritual that's all that matters. The neo-pagans tried to evangelise Dave with their brand of new age spirituality and the ex-Hindu asked questions after question. Many issues were gently probed by razor-sharp minds that managed to stay lucid after more alcohol than should have been possible. This was not an event that Dave organised or initiated, he just had enjoyed previous conversations with his friend Andy and was happy to accept an invitation. The setting was not forced and because everyone felt relaxed and comfortable the conversations were open and profound.

Charity Dinners

Charitable events are hugely popular. Marie Curie Cancer Care suggest holding dinner parties and charging £5 per head, on the basis that three guests will raise funds for one hour of nursing care (£15) for a cancer patient. Look out for other suggestions like these on television and in the press that could be adapted to your social circle.

Consider throwing simple fun suppers like pizza or pancake parties to launch the start of Lent, and ask everyone to bring fillings and topping ingredients.

> '**There comes a time in every woman's life when the only thing to drink is champagne.**'
> **Bette Davis**

A Champagne moment

Wine tasting or cheese and wine evenings have been regularly used in an informal setting as a way of getting people together, so why not try champagne?

When is the right time to have a champagne moment? Many people appeared to have one at the Good Food Show in Birmingham, surrounded by Jamie Oliver, Gordon Ramsay and Ainsley Harriott!

A recent evening held in Chester commenced with an informal talk on the history of champagne and its production; and then they tasted and shared a few bottles together.

A champagne tasting event may not be for everyone so it is probably helpful to do your homework first. Champagne is expensive and viewed as a treat so it may be that you would wish to combine the event with another activity.

How could you develop this idea to suit your group of friends? A champagne breakfast with a speaker linked to the theme of celebration. Or perhaps a strawberries and champagne event linked to Wimbledon.

Murder Mystery Evenings

Or how about hosting a murder dinner? These were very popular twenty years ago and have come round again. These are great fun and there are lots of these on the market at the moment for about £15 - £20, or look out for a box at your local charity shop. Once you've done a few you might even be confident enough to write your own. You can also download games catering for groups as small as 6 and as large as 200 from www.murdermysterygames.co.uk

The game boxes usually contain invitations, recipe ideas and all the items you need to run the evening, including a taped message from the Inspector and a running programme of hints and tips for each role.

There are lots of different ways to have fun in a murder mystery evening, and you'd be amazed at the different side of people that comes out when they are in costume and playing a role. It's a great way to break the ice with neighbours and friends.

For slightly larger events you can go to an organised event in a hotel.

These take place around the country; some hotels even run them as murder weekends. At these events each table constitutes a team who act as detectives and observe vital clues throughout the evening. The action is played out throughout the evening between courses. At the end of the evening the cast come into the room and they are summoned to each table in turn to be interrogated. The cast then judge the tables for who worked well as a team and how pertinent the questions were.

You might try organising an event like this yourself and bringing in a team of actors to entertain you with a murder played out in your midst. The best arrangement is a circle of tables of up to 10 people with a space in the middle for the drama. The group will advise you of a suitable programme for the night. This is a unique combination of theatre, improvisation and audience involvement for groups up to 120. Obviously there is a fee involved but people will usually be happy to pay for a ticket to such a fun evening – especially if there is good food thrown in. Guaranteed to provide a talking point afterwards. www.themurdersquad.co.uk

"Tea is drunk to forget the din of the world"

Tien Yiheng

Afternoon Tea

Afternoon tea is making a comeback, so dig out your pretty china and scone recipes. Scour the charity shops for individual patterened tea cups and saucers. Hotels now charge more for events that incude vintage tea sets, so recreate the latest trend in your own home! Supermarkets sell tiered cake stands in cardboard or plastic that are very inexpensive.

Quartered sandwiches on different colours of bread, miniature scones, tiny slices of cake and strawberries make for a delicious spread. Concentrate on small tasty portions and simple fresh food. It's an inexpensive way of entertaining and everyone gets home before dark.

Why not sample some of the herbal and 'posh' teas on sale in the shops? Simple cakes can be bought from the supermarket and icing, fruit or chocolate added. It might be an ideal time for your craft or reading group to meet on a Saturday or Sunday or during the week if the members are not out at work.

Jesus recognised the value of eating with friends and that people are more relaxed and more receptive to new ideas when they are eating, so food played a major part in his ministry.

The details of our Holy Communion rituals were set out after a Passover meal. The challenging question, 'Who do people say I am?' was asked during a fish barbecue on the beach. And Jesus chose to pitch some of his most potent teaching during the Feast of Tabernacles when the crowds would be at maximum capacity. When he fed 5000 they turned up in droves the next day to hear him.

People love to be fed – and attendance at events is always higher when there is food included.

So why not open up your dining room, get some assistance from Delia, and see what God can do with your guests through the conversations you have?

The Library

Few homes are grand enough to have a library, but most of us in the free world have a collection of books and a quiet place in our homes to curl up and read. Freedom to read can be limited by the demands of a busy career, caring for children or the elderly and for some people, reading will never be a pleasure, always a chore. For some of us it could be that we feel an unexplained sense of unease for reading during the day, as experienced by this literary character:

'Lady Peabury was in the morning room reading a novel: early training gave a guilty spice to this recreation, for she had been brought up to believe that to read a novel before luncheon was one of the gravest sins it was possible for a gentlewoman to commit'.

Evelyn Waugh 1903-1966

This rule must still be written on our consciences, because hands up anyone who feels guilty while reading a chapter of a novel during daylight hours when there are still chores to be done, or a stacked in-tray to be dealt with? But if it really was for freedom that Christ has set us free, then we should allow ourselves a little relaxation.

UNLOCKING THE DOOR

Activate Your Life

> '**There is no surer foundation for a beautiful friendship than a mutual taste in literature.**'
>
> **P G Wodehouse**

Alice Through the Locking Glass

TO KILL A LOCKING BIRD

50 TYPES OF LOCK - MANDY CATTO

LOCK WHO'S TALKING – J. MCQUOID

Brian's Story

At a 40th birthday party Brian got into conversation with a young man he had not met before. Within minutes this young man began explaining how he had recently been thinking a great deal about the broader, deeper questions of life – 'what was it all about, what was the purpose of doing what we do and is this all there is?'

After a lengthy conversation that touched on church, the Bible, Christians and God as well as all the relevant abuses and negative impressions, the young man asked if Brian knew of a good book he could read to get him started on the journey of investigating faith. He didn't want anything "too Godly" he insisted, no Bible! Brian said he had just the book and a few days later passed on a copy of "Long Journey Home" by Os Guinness. Sometimes, we need to trust God that books might take someone's faith further without us being present.

Reading Groups

The Reading Group was possibly inspired by the Holy Spirit as a wonderful forum for sharing your faith without the aid of a soapbox. Secular books are full of issues of morality, choices, life and death and loneliness and you'll have some brilliant opportunities to share some of your views.

Reading, according to the 2004 General Household Survey for the Office of National Statistics, is the latest craze to sweep Britain, yet it's been around for thousands of years. Reading is now the fourth most popular leisure activity in the country and frequent discussions of the latest novels on daytime TV shows and sitcoms has led neighbours around the country to get together and discuss their favourites.

When the BBC launched The Big Read it was an opportunity for the public to vote for their favourite book, culminating in a top ten debate, with star names championing the literary rivals. The public's top 100 books were revealed, launching several months of reading activity during which people were encouraged to swap and talk about their favourite reads. The top ten books were featured, with ten programmes profiling each book in depth. The BBC2 Controller, Jane Root, hoped the idea would catch the public imagination and inspire people to set up book clubs up and down the country. "We are trying to turn a private experience into something people do together. I have this fantasy that you get on the tube in the morning and everyone is reading the same book".

This vision has recently been taken up in Liverpool where there was a campaign to get everyone reading the book 'Holes'. The local libraries stocked up on it and bookshops were offering big reductions. The hope was that people would buy a copy and then leave it on a bus or park bench and someone who couldn't afford to buy one could then pick it up – making the project accessible to everyone.

A helpful site is www.damaris.org, which reviews current books, films and music and includes discussion questions. Meet in homes, coffee bars, and pubs – anywhere the group feel comfortable. If you can't find anyone who shares your passion for reading, put a note up in the local library – it'll give you a chance to meet fellow bookworms. Allowing everyone a chance to choose the book and chair the discussions will widen your horizons this year.

The group select a book to read over an agreed period of time. Then get together and discuss it, if you felt you could identify with the main characters, the plot, anything that struck you as a crisis point in the story – where a different decision would have totally changed the outcome, etc. You decide what to talk about.

'What is the use of a book, thought Alice, without pictures or conversations.'

Lewis Carroll, Alice's Adventures in Wonderland

Lots of newspapers and magazines offer 'Book of the Month' suggestions. Tapping in 'Reading Groups' on the Internet brings up a wide selection of websites with hints, tips and book reviews.
Try www.readinggroupguides.com as a helpful starter.

Many women who meet other mums at the school gate have found a reading group meeting in each other's houses is a great way of getting to know each other better. Take it in turns to host, provide simple snacks and choose the next book. A quick text round two days before the next meet is usually enough to keep everyone connected.

Some book group favourites are 'We need to talk about Kevin' by Lionel Shriver, 'The Curious Incident of the Dog in the Night-Time' by Mark Haddon, 'Me Before You' by Jojo Moyes, 'The Best Exotic Marigold Hotel' by Deborah Moggach, 'Call the Midwife' by Jennifer Worth, 'Still Alice' by Lisa Genoa and 'The Shack' by William P Young. These were favourites, not because everyone liked them, but because they stimulated the most interesting discussions and gripped the attention of a diverse group.

If you are in a group, be open-minded and prepared to have a go at reading books that wouldn't normally read. You may be surprised at how many different books you come to enjoy, or at least be intrigued by and listening to others' appreciation can influence and widen your interest. And the discussions that flow out of the books will encompass issues of life, growth, suffering, eternity, purpose and meaning. You don't have to chip in with a suggestion of a Christian book every few months, maybe just a particular favourite of yours with great themes just when it is your turn. Meaningful conversations will happen anyway.

The **Bathroom**

'I can't think of any sorrow in the world that a hot bath wouldn't help, just a little'

Susan Glasse

In a recent UK survey, eight out of ten women said they wished they could change their lives and according to statistics the experience of a mundane and tiring existence is driving women to hit the bottle and raid the fridge in an attempt to de-stress. Each generation seems to struggle with its own crippling health and social problems and as we look at the lives of 21st century women it seems that stress is one of the top ranking problems of our time.

So any de-stressing ideas are sure to prove popular, not only with us but also with the women we work and live near. A one-off event or a series covering stress related issues is something that's sure to be welcomed in any area as long as it's timed to fit in with women's busy schedules.

One group organised a couple of successful Saturday morning workshops under the title 'Understanding Yourself'. They covered themes such as 'How to cope with stress', 'How to build your self esteem', 'How to communicate effectively' and 'How to break free from being a people pleaser'. Sessions like these would be relevant to both men and women.

Julie's Story

After many years of not having to go to work Julie found herself, after the recession and some difficult family issues, looking for a job. She occasionally attended a beauty spa and was asked by the receptionist if she would be interested in working there part-time, administering a light treatment for weight loss. She accepted and began working the light machine as women lay on the couch for an hour at a time, usually over six weeks. As a good listener, and someone genuinely interested in other people, she found that her clients opened up and talked honestly about their lives, their concerns and their disappointments. She talked gently and openly about her faith and how Jesus had helped her to face life's difficulties. And as she talked, time after time, 'Jesus showed up, right there in the treatment room'. One of her clients, Dee, arrived in a very unhappy and cynical state. She began to share and listen and agreed to come along with Julie to try out the local church. She loved it and now never misses a week, attending every service and Bible study possible.

Julie has found that the job she wasn't sure she wanted, has become her ministry and enabled her to meet and reach out to women she would never have the opportunity to cross paths with. She carries with her a Bible and devotional as she never knows when she will get an opportunity to share, not just the light slimming treatment, but the Light of the World.

Spa Parties

Spa Parties, pampering events and make-overs can all give the opportunity of meaningful conversations in a relaxed atmosphere, when women will often talk openly about some of the issues they're struggling with. These can be home grown events, even using store cupboard ingredients or bring in the experts using party plans like Neal's Yard or Body Shop at Home.

Most stress busting articles include the suggestion of 'setting aside some quiet time', to balance the noise and confusion which infiltrates much of our time so biblical meditation, prayer or reading a few verses from a modern version of the Bible are ideas which could work for many listeners, if presented gently and in the right context.

The bathroom is a great place to unwind, especially if you have a good selection of beauty products to pour into a deep bath, and there are so many wonderful products to choose from even in the budget ranges. Beauty is big business and this area accounts for the vast majority of spending by women.

Working women with children might have a lot less to spend on themselves, and with so many single mums around, how about arranging a more domestic version of pampering? Even gathering a few friends into your home and giving each other a facial and a manicure would be a welcome offer. It's a great time for a heart to heart. Many beauty therapists and hairdressers report that they often end up as amateur counsellors because clients pour out their troubles as well as their good news when they relax.

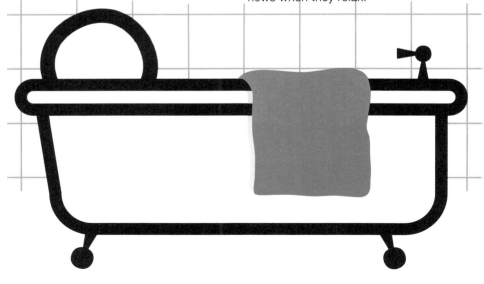

Play some relaxing music and offer low-fat nibbles and flavoured mineral water. Perhaps you could read some inspirational poetry or a short piece from the Bible while everyone is wearing a face pack. Using a title like Miracle Morning might open up some interesting opportunities!

Consider having a pamper night using cosmetics homemade out of store cupboard ingredients, just like granny used to do it! Cleanse and tone your skin with lavender vinegar, and put on a homemade facemask and pop a slice of cucumber over each eye, lie back and listen to some soothing music and maybe read an inspirational poem to finish. One of the most humble services one person can do for another is to wash their feet. So give someone a special treat by giving them a refreshing footbath and a pedicure.

Nail Bars are the latest salons to appear on the high street and if you've ever walked past one when shopping you'll see women sitting for hours while the nail technician transforms her hands. Could you do a basic manicure course so that you get lots of opportunity for a one-to-one with people?

Sarah Stacey (editor of www.beautybible.com) organized a team of therapists to come to her home for a 'Heaven at Home' party. Stacey and her five friends put on bath robes and sipped strawberry smoothies while the team got to work with a mixture of facials, massages, manicures, pedicures and waxing. They even had a bartender to serve drinks and nibbles and the only fingers they lifted were the ones being manicured.

Health Spas

A trip to a health spa is always popular, so consider planning a day, or even longer away. Dawn spent a 'top to toe' day with some of her neighbours, at a large hotel. While they were sitting in the jacuzzi, chatting, one of the group began to ask Dawn some quite deep questions about her faith. Eight women joined in the conversation, until after half an hour they all emerged from the water looking a little prune-like. So often we believe that sharing our faith will be difficult, yet so often God uses the fun, natural events of ordinary living to allow some life changing conversations to take place.

Typing 'health spa' into a search engine like 'Google' should bring up some venues in your area.

'The Esther Group'

A group of women from the Heaton area of Newcastle attended an Activate event in Gateshead, and were inspired by the ideas that seemed to speak right into their desire to serve their community. So after a few 'get togethers' and much prayer, 'Esther' was formed. Originally the team brought their caring skills into the homes of Christian women who invited their friends along for a pamper evening. Esther quickly 'found favour with all the people' and the team soon had a diary full of bookings.

Two years later the Esther group is still committed to the vision, though they have had a few changes of members. They are led by Margaret (a hairdresser) and the team now consists of Sarah (who offers hand massage), Louise (face massage) Karen (make-up), Carol (nails) and Audrey (also a hairdresser). The difference now is that the group has contacted several local welfare projects and the recipients of these beauty treatments are vulnerable women on the margins of society.

Some are living on the streets. Sarah finds that some women struggle at first with her hand massage treatment because of the intimate nature of the touching: "Some of these girls do not have anybody in their lives and they are just not used to being loved. We are very up front about being Christians and we assure them that Jesus loves them. It's up to them to take it further if they want to talk deeply.
The heartfelt thanks and comments are very touching. The places we visit include 'The People's Kitchen' which is a place that provides food, clothing and friendship to disadvantaged people in Newcastle and Gateshead.

We also visit locations run by the Aquila Housing Association, which help homeless young women in all circumstances. We try to introduce the evening by telling the women about Esther and why we are doing it. Then follows an evening of laughter, sometimes tears but always blessings from the Lord.

The women who we see are usually young and have traumatic histories. However, they never fail to amaze us with how strong and determined they are and how much they have to give. We never 'preach' to them but are open to talking about our faith. Often we find that they are extremely receptive and open to listening about Jesus. Some have even had experience of Him personally. For some of these women it may be the first time anyone has touched them in a non-threatening way, or bothered to show them that they are loved.

Once a year we hold an Esther day. This has been run on 3 occasions and has proved to be extremely successful with some women giving their lives to God following it. It is a day with talks on various women's issues and a Christian speaker. Being part of the team has blessed me in so many ways. Being able to show Jesus' love to these women through our touch or listening skills is such a privilege. We are a close team who pray regularly about Esther and for the Holy Sprit to work through us making a difference to these women."

These evenings are about Jesus' love for everyone and Philippians 2:3 that tells of this says, 'Do nothing out of selfish ambition or vain conceit, but in humility consider others better than yourselves'.

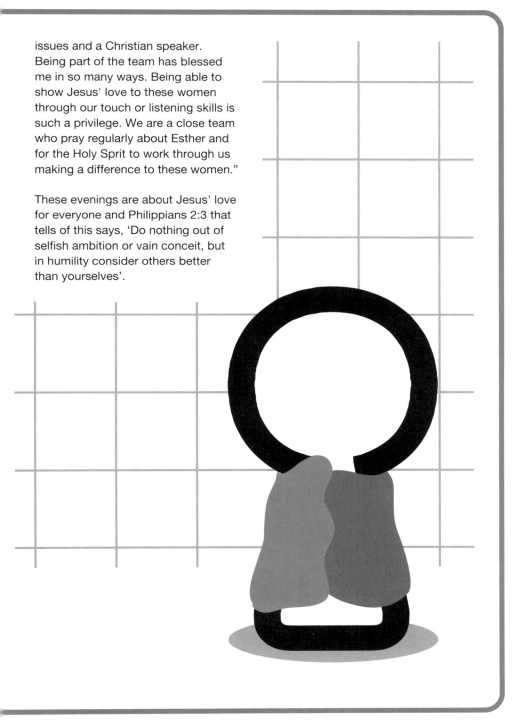

Working from Home

There is a growing trend for people to work from home, and lots of modern houses contain a study. If you can have a break occasionally why not send brief encouraging emails to other busy friends? It's important to keep in touch, or your solitary workplace can be isolating and will dull your creativity.

Drive down almost any motorway in the country and you'll spot signs in fields about the benefits of working from home. Certainly the increased traffic jams make commuting a nightmare and the working day so much longer. The thought of rolling out of bed and

into the office is very attractive – especially if you are caring for children, aged parents or pets and require flexibility in your working hours.

The advent of Broadband means that many homes have high-speed Internet access allowing home-workers to send and receive emails all day long without clogging up the phone line. With the help of a good computer the home office can be as efficient as an office in the average workplace.

There are some pitfalls though. Domestic issues can distract you. Though you can happily put a wash - load in the machine while waiting for the kettle to

The Study

'One of the symptoms of an approaching nervous breakdown is the belief that one's work is terribly important.' Bertrand Russell

boil, the ironing pile is ever before you when you work from home. Though it's great to be able to go to the school carol service or sports day to watch your children taking part, it's inevitable that other parents forget that you are actually working and consider that you are always available to chat or to bail them out when they need someone to help at the Christmas Fair or other such event. It can also be a lonely life without the stimulation of other colleagues to 'bat ideas about', so keep in touch with others as much as possible by phone or email.

On the upside you can be available when people really need you and that is a great feeling. Being there for someone in a crisis can be a huge privilege and will often give you the opportunity to listen and to pray with someone. God uses people who are willing and available. You can be around for the family and go for a lunchtime dog walk. A great opportunity to chat with someone as you walk side-by-side and good exercise as well. You can always make up your hours after dark when you might well have been travelling home anyway!

Home workers can be part of an online community who aim to support one another. This is a great opportunity as it 'expands your territory' and widens your circle of influence without having to leave the house. Log on to www.homeworking.com

The Workplace

If you work away from home, it could well be that the workplace is the environment where you spend most of your time. When we talk about doing things in the community and reaching out to neighbours we mean it in the widest possible sense, and for you, community and neighbours might mean the people you work with. So consider what you might do to bring God's love into the workplace. If people are interested in faith issues you could run a lunchtime Alpha, but for other colleagues you might need to be a little more creative in order to identify their needs and bring God's love into those situations. Do log onto the LICC website for helpful work related articles, resources and events (www.licc.org.uk).

Many in the business world have found inspiration from Laurie Beth Jones's book 'Jesus CEO' (Hyperion Books – ISBN 0-7868-8126-7). One director of a large multi-national company said, 'Who would have thought that by living like Jesus you could be successful?'. This is a book, which could be lent or given to a work colleague who may read it and find that the Bible has a lot to say about the issues they're facing.

For computer users who want to explore the Christian faith anonymously there are excellent websites available that are contemporary, creative and very professionally produced. Try directing your friends to **www.church.co.uk** or **www.rejesus.co.uk**

Facebook

Since Mark Zuckerberg started his university social networking site in 2004 the world has downloaded and connected in an unprecedented way.

Addictive? Time wasting? Potentially, but like any other modern media, Facebook holds endless opportunites for good. Make your profile match your life, put on your favourite verse as an update, tag yourself at church events, post pictures of your church family having fun. People are used to seeing others share their lives and activities on a daily basis.

What an opportunity to share your faith naturally, with humour and in a positive light. Event invitations are embedded so put your dates of events, photos of the location and a biography of your speaker on, choosing which of your facebook friends to invite.

No pressure, no embarrassment, just a normal invite along with others they will receive for dancing shows and school discos.

Kumar's Story

Kumar became a Christian in his early forties and had a wide circle of non-churched friends who he found it completely natural to talk with about the excitement of his new found faith.

As a facebook fan (or perhaps addict), it was a logical step to weave his new faith into his facebook persona. Photos, events, funny stories, new challenges all found their way onto the inboxes of his hundreds of facebook friends. He is always on the lookout for new YouTube clips that will entertain as well as bring in a great message about Jesus. Last Christmas he 'liked' a clip from a modern day shepherd in Bethlehem that led his facebook friends to watch four minutes of the reality of who Jesus is, without a word of jargon and no hint of cringe.

He is a facebook evangelist. The social networking world needs more like him.

'Facebook has more than 1 billion members, which by population makes it the third largest country in the world- somewhere between India and the United States. Who's sending missionaries to that country? Who's planting churches there?'
Phil Cooke

Photography

As Estelle walked across the bridge near her home in Chester one evening she was fascinated to see a group of around thirty people, all with tripods, photographing the moon on the river. Always open to new ideas, Estelle realised the potential in holding a photographic evening in her home. A recommendation by a friend, soon after, of a young Sheffield photographer called Jodi, led Estelle to organising a fascinating evening at her home.

About fifty guests, from different backgrounds, crowded into Estelle's lounge and watched a delightful visual presentation of lifestyle photography. Beginning with 'tips for amateurs' Jodi showed how to ensure that the most flattering pictures possible are taken, by getting the lighting right and placing the subject at a slight angle for a narrower frame, and how to make people look smaller and taller. Very helpful advice for amateurs. She then went on to show a sequence of wedding photos. Relating some potentially disastrous episodes at her first wedding shoot, kept the guests amused.

As Jodi said, 'Photography has the ability to record not just how we look but how we feel and where we are in a particular stage of life. Photographs taken in your own environment allow each image to tell a story, reminding you of your home, and your surroundings. It's the endless possibilities that holding a camera affords for creativity and fun and by the desire to produce works for individuals that they will cherish and value, that will be about them. It's the power that the visual image has to capture a stolen moment of tenderness, and to record people as they are known, and underpinning all this, is the truth and inspiration of the Christian message of Jesus – I have found him to be the most singularly inspiring, challenging, gracious and authoritative individual I have ever met. He continues to shape everything I do'.

With the increasing popularity of digital cameras, making it ever easier to download our photos onto computer, could you plan a photographic event locally, either in your home or another suitable venue?

> ## "A good snapshot keeps a moment from running away."
> **Eudora Welty**

happy times...

Stress

Recent medical and technological advances have not been able to rid society of health issues and social problems. As we look at the lives of 21st Century men and women it seems that stress might be one of the top ranking problems of our time. A survey by First Choice Travel revealed that one in five British workers would not take his or her full holiday entitlement this year – because of stress. Up to three million full-time workers stay at the office because they are scared of losing their jobs or are simply too busy. 50% of the female and 40% of the male workforce complain that they are living to work, rather than working to live. It should come as no surprise, therefore, that The Confederation of British Industry (CBI) has estimated that stress and mental health problems cost employers £7 billion a year in sick pay, lost production and costs to the NHS.

Social Trends indicate that 70% of women are working, and within this group there are more full-time than part-time employees, and 20% of women are queuing at the doctor's surgery because of fatigue, sleep problems, irritability and anxiety. The major causes of these stress-related problems are cited as home, family, and career and juggling all three.

An article in the Daily Mail interviewed Jill and Sue from Kent. Both executives with children and busy husbands, their lives are organized like clockwork in order to stay afloat. Up at dawn, they juggle school runs, music lessons, sports, child-minders, housework and shopping with incredible efficiency. When the school rang Jill to say one of her children was ill and needed collecting the system broke down. Nobody else was available to help and she had three appointments in her diary. "In the end I had to put off my appointments and rush to the school. On the train I felt so stressed that I thought about opening the door and throwing myself out".

Women who work to this extent may only have Sunday as a rest day – church will have to seem a very valuable option for them to give up their very precious free time. How can we come alongside them and bless them? And when is the best time to plan something?

Debt

Managing money is something that many people struggle with, but there are those for whom spiralling debt is a crippling issue. It can cause depression, despair, family breakdown or even suicide.

Could you help by organizing Debt counselling in your area? Christians Against Poverty (CAP) are a national charity, working across the UK to lift people out of poverty and debt. They offer free debt counselling through a network of 233 centres based in local churches. The CAP Money Course is a revolutionary money management course that teaches people budgeting skills and a simple, cash-based system that really works. This course will help anyone to get more in control of their finances, so they can budget, save and prevent debt. For more information about CAP and about running a CAP Money Course visit their website on **www.capuk.org**

Redundancy/unemployment

Redundancy and unemployment can happen to anyone. They usually come about because a firm has financial problems and needs to make hard decisions, but it's inevitable that the person losing their job will take it personally. This can result in a feeling of rejection and isolation, which can easily spiral into low self-esteem and depression.

If you become aware of someone in this position you might be able to help in many ways. First of all to help them to think positively and consider what they would really like to do. Often the thing we most dread can turn out to be the thing which liberates us, and losing a job might be the push we need to find something more stimulating or even more financially rewarding.

Why not see if you can help the person to think objectively about their personal strengths and skills? Perhaps using something like the Gallup 'Strengthsfinder' and then construct a new tailored CV which specifically majors on those strengths. Being accountable to a friend might be the encouragement they need to keep on posting those letters and filling in applications.

You might do this as an individual or alternatively your church or Christian group could offer this as a service in your local community. Perhaps even making a room with a computer available to people who don't have that facility at home. Above all, your support will help them to maintain their self-esteem and confidence, which are both crucial factors when job-hunting.

If you're the person who is out of work, look for opportunities that aren't available to you when you're working. It may be that your circle of influence changes dramatically when you cease to be part of the workforce. If you know of others in the same situation as you, starting a support group might be appropriate. There may be activities in your local area that you can become part of for a time, giving the chance to make new relationships with those you meet in these new situations.

The Bedroom

'Laugh and the world laughs with you; snore and you sleep alone'

Anthony Burgess' 'Inside Mr Enderby' - 1963

Clothes

Some people are very happy to turn out their wardrobes every season and make a trip to the charity shop but most of us hoard clothes for years with the intention of slimming into them or finding something to go with random articles of clothing we bought on impulse. Swapping clothes with friends is a great way of acquiring new outfits.

Sarah, a fashion designer in London has regular 'Swishing' parties. Friends gather over afternoon tea or evening drinks and barter. Everyone brings nice, clean, presentable clothes that are lurking unloved in their wardrobe, and other girls fall in love with them and give them a good home. People might bring one sweater and take home two pairs of shoes, or hang a party frock on the 'Swishing Rail' and take a pair of skinny jeans and feather boa. It's a great way to spend an afternoon with friends without hitting the credit card, you get some 'new' clothes into the bargain, and it is eco-friendly. At a time of financial austerity, this appeals to many people. For more information visit www.swishing.com

Fashion show

If you want to put on a bigger event, why not consider a fashion show?

A local designer outlet might be willing to put this on for you if you can guarantee an audience and a good location. They'll probably distribute tickets among their customers to boost your numbers. This kind of event draws a large crowd if you do it well. You can easily hire smoke machines, and with a bit of catwalk staging and some music and good lighting it will look very professional. Why not include a glass of champagne and a posh chocolate for an extra treat?

Charge an entrance fee to cover costs and give the profits to a local charity for an extra feel-good factor.

One group concluded their fashion show with a five minute talk entitled 'Is God in fashion?'.

Colour session

Impulse buying is greatly reduced after you've had a colour consultation and is almost as popular with men as it is with women. The consultant will look at skin tone, eyes and hair colour and help identify the range of colours that suit you best. Often they will supply a swatch of your best colours to assist you when shopping. That way you'll know that anything you buy will match the things already in your wardrobe, and extend the range of your outfits by helping you mix and match what you already have. You might even be tempted to try colours that you've never worn before and discover a whole new look.

This works best in a small group, where people can encourage each other and get some experience of what to look for. A Colour session can be fun, it deepens your relationship with people and (if you invite a Christian colour consultant) it can be an opportunity for a gentle evangelistic message. It also brings the tantalising potential of a whole new wardrobe. This sounds expensive – but you can always get together with your newly colour conscious friends and pool resources.

Sex and Relationships

The Bible is very matter-of-fact about sexuality, but in polite Christian circles we mostly avoid talking about it. It's so easy to skirt round or gloss over these issues. But maybe being willing to address them and give a Christian perspective might bring opportunities for evangelism. Somebody once said that minds were like parachutes – they have to be open to be any good! So what is an appropriate response to a generation that already sees Christianity as irrelevant and God as some forbidding killjoy who disapproves of everything they do?

Well actually, sex was God's idea in the first place. Surely, when he told Adam & Eve to be fruitful and multiply this was a Garden of Eden colloquialism for sex. And they certainly took him at his word, as did their descendants after them. The Old Testament is full of people begetting all over the place!

Solomon was reputedly a great lover, and what is Song of Songs if not a touch of carefully coded eroticism? Maybe the Bible would be the last place we'd expect to find this kind of material, and possibly that is why some have questioned the place of this book within the Old Testament.

Commenting on the imagery in Song of Songs for the Church of England Newspaper, Catherine Fox said, "Modern day couples might require certain marital aids such as a map of the female form with helpful arrows and informative labels such as 'flock of goats descending from Mount Gilead' or 'halves of a pomegranate.'"

Distinguished Christian psychiatrist Jack Dominian published a book Let's Make Love, subtitled 'the meaning of sexual intercourse' in which he concludes that the church has bound itself into a negative view of this gift of God's good creation. He commends sex as deeply personal and relational, even reflecting the character of God in a mysterious way.

The front covers of the best selling magazines which adorn our newsagents' shelves, deal with some aspect of sex in almost every issue. This must lead us to conclude that it's a subject that people are very interested in. What a tragedy that we are surrounded daily with TV programmes, art, film and even real life stories sold to magazines and newspapers, that champion casual sex and pornography.

Just where does that dividing line between loving affection and eroticism lie? And does it matter anyway in a loving relationship? Where do people look for sensible answers to these and countless other questions about sexuality?

It might seem an adventurous subject to tackle, but if it's done sensibly and with sensitivity it would be a great way of breaking down the myths

'I know nothing about sex because I was always married'

Zsa Zsa Gabor

about Christ, Christians and the church, and would provide a natural forum for the sharing of faith.

The Romance Academy is a revolutionary relationships project that tackles teen pregnancy and under-age sex head on. Through their 14 week programme they address the underlying causes of risky youth behaviour such as poor self-esteem, low aspirations and lack of positive family and community life by promoting the value of stable relationships. For more information on running a course visit www.romanceacademy.org

Listening

A bedroom should be a place of tranquillity, where you can relax and be yourself, where you can sleep well and wake up feeling refreshed and revitalised to face the challenges of a new day. Sadly, all too often this is not the case. 19% of women are regularly visiting their doctor, suffering with symptoms of stress. Some of them are struggling with depression, so that getting up in the morning is a major hurdle, and even just tackling everyday domestic things is exhausting and draining.

Can you come alongside someone with depression and take some of the physical burdens from them? And if you don't feel qualified to give the right advice – be the friend who listens. Listening attentively without commenting, advising or judging is hugely valuable. A helping hand with chores, shopping or collecting children might make all the difference.

Sometimes exercise helps, so plan a walk in a local park or woodland. Some counselling centres offer depression self-help groups. Even an invitation to join a discussion group or reading group might give a lift and provide a focus in a dull week.

Divorce

Over a third of households comprise just one person living alone.

This can be a young professional person who has chosen not to marry just yet, or who has not yet met a 'significant other', or it can be brought about by divorce or death, both of which are forms of bereavement. Facilitating a Divorce Recovery group might be helpful or just being willing to support a colleague going through divorce may be what's most needed. HTB have produced a course 'Recovering from Divorce or Separation' which includes a video set and a course manual. The video includes tips for those running their own course.

Further details from Alpha resources – 0845 644 7533 or visit www.rdscourse.org.uk. The book, 'Tracing the Rainbow' (see right) has helpful guidelines on divorce too.

A divorce is like an amputation; you survive but there's less of you

Margaret Attwood

Bereavement

'Tracing the Rainbow' by Pablo Martinez and Ali Hull gives practical advice and understanding which will help in coming alongside those who have lost loved ones through death or divorce. There's help in enabling us to understand grief in its various forms and it encourages us to look at how we can help, and avoid hindering, as we try and comfort people.

In cases of divorce and death there can be frequent bouts of loneliness. A sense of disconnectedness, and a feeling that the world goes on around us but without us. All too often, people who live alone are never included in invitations to dinner parties or outings. They sometimes feel that they are seen as a threat to other people's relationships.

So, many of the activities in this book are ideal for inviting people on their own. Do look at the people around you and be aware of those who live alone. Take the risk of inviting them to join in; even if they say no they'll probably appreciate being asked.

The Nursery

Informal Discussion

Ask a group of Mums, over a cup of coffee, whilst the children are playing to give their view on the following quote:

'Many parents do nothing about their children's religious education, telling them they can decide what to believe when they're 18. That's like telling them they can decide when they're 18 whether to brush their teeth or not. By then their teeth may well have fallen out. Likewise, their principles and morality may be non-existent.'

Princess Grace of Monaco

Baby Music - Julie's Story

Julie, the leader says, "When I first presented the idea of Babysong in a church service, all I asked for was that people in the congregation would pray for the work and for the families that would come. Within a few weeks I was given instruments, offers of help to make the drinks and most importantly prayer support. I now have five church members praying for Babysong on a Friday and it gives me peace and confidence that all we do is protected by God and held in his love and that he leads and directs as I prepare and look ahead.

Babysong is wonderful and here are a few things that I thank God for as I look back on two years of Babysong:

- Being the creator who makes me creative as I plan the programme

- Making it easy to share my faith in the songs and in chats over coffee

- The excitement I see in each child's face and body as we sing their name

- The way the children use the music day to day at home

- A music teacher's joy of seeing toddlers marching crotchets, jogging quavers, walking minims, sitting and standing, simply by listening to the piano

- A 3-year-old boy on his second visit tugging my shirt saying "Lisa, I want to see your church"

- A mum saying "This is the highlight of my week"

- Parents getting to know each other and walking up to town for lunch at the end of Babysong

- Money raised for the work of the Salvation Army across the world but also for the witness it is to the parents that them coming also helps further afield

- A letter from a mum saying how Babysong has changed their lives and how even daddy knows which song to use to soothe a crying baby or to get a job done

- The privilege of getting to know families and being able to support them in prayer".

Dad & Me

Toddler groups are popular in every town and village throughout the country, but the Dads might like to consider a different take on the traditional group. One Mum in Kent asked, 'Why isn't there something like a toddler group for dads to give us a break now and again?' This sparked the beginning of 'Just Daddy and Me'. Meeting on one Saturday the end. One dad said, 'I got up at five o'clock this morning to get the two girls ready for this!!' Bear in mind they start at ten o'clock!

The benefits from the group are many. The mums have said how much they appreciate the time, some meet for coffee, some have gone for a facial or just a quiet wander round town without a little person in tow. The dads are also very appreciative

'why isn't there something like a toddler group for dads to give us a break now and again?'

morning a month as many as thirty-six Dads have attended in a week. It gives Mums a break, and is a place where young Dads can meet up with others in a similar position. They can also observe their little ones interact with other children in a way they don't usually have the opportunity to do. It's an opportunity to build bridges and friendships through which there's sometimes an opportunity to share the good news of the love of Jesus.

In practical terms, the hall set up, is just the same as the Mums and Tots group: the baby area, craft area, book corner, Wendy House, large apparatus and ride and toy area. Rather than start with a story and song time, due to the fact that some of the Dads stroll in a little late, we have the song time at of the opportunity. At the end of one song time, one of the Dads remarked, 'I've never seen that side of my daughter's character before'. She had just sung a solo into the microphone for us because she knew different words to 'Twinkle, Twinkle...'. One Mum reported back on a Tuesday that her husband had told her 'I never thought I'd hear myself singing songs about Jesus'.

These Saturdays are really wonderful times. There's a very lively buzz of male conversations, shared play-time between Dad and little one. Also the children have a safe environment in which to explore on their own before coming back to check up on Dad. A number of families have begun to attend the family services at the church as a result of this activity.

The particular value of reaching out to Dads can be seen by considering this statistic:

- If a child is the first member of the family to become a Christian, approximately 3.5% of families follow

  - If a Mum is the first person of the family to become a Christian, then about 17% of families follow

  - However, if a Dad is the first of the family to become a Christian, a startling 93% of families follow!

www.whychurch.org.uk

The Children's Room

Being a parent is tricky, and there's no chance of a dress rehearsal. The encouraging news is that other people around you will be feeling just like you do, so there's no need to struggle in silence. As Sir Peter Ustinov said, 'Parents are the bones on which children sharpen their teeth'.

'We spend the first twelve months of our children's lives teaching them to walk and talk, and the next twelve telling them to sit down and shut up.'

Phyllis Diller - US Comedian

Parenting Groups

Sharing difficulties, failures and successes will help you, and help others. So why not consider gathering some other parents around you to start a support group? If the other people are the parents of your child's friends then so much the better – you can put up a united front over issues when they try out the age-old line, "Everybody else can, why can't I?"

Positive Parenting and Care for the Family have both produced excellent materials to help guide your group through a course together, for more information visit www.parenting.org.uk

Joy's Story

Joy and a group of friends began a parenting course, mainly with parents who were not church attenders. They met in a home for six weeks and together used the material provided. The leader just facilitated the group and didn't act as an expert nor did the other parents look to her for answers. The video clips and parents' handbook provided plenty of discussion material, which gave freedom for lively discussion and disagreement without causing offence.

There was time for reflection and relaxation at the end of each session. Joy found the first two courses easy to lead with lots of fun and laughter, particularly during the role-play.

However, a word of caution. Christian parents made up the majority at the third course Joy led and she found this group were far more opinionated and appeared less willing to consider or learn from the experiences of others!

It would be wise to ensure that any Christians attending the group are sensitive to the difficulties that some of the other participants may be facing.

Schools

'A teacher affects eternity; he can never tell where his influence stops'
Henry Brookes Adams 1838-1918

A great many wars are held in the classroom. As students recognise the limits of the teacher's authority, and discipline levels erode, more and more teachers are abandoning the profession, and those who do stay can often feel demoralised. Now, more than ever, they need the support of parents to affirm them. This could be done through joining the PTA, keeping in constant touch with the establishment where children spend most of their weekdays, and fundraising to ensure that the children have access to the best possible facilities.

Parents are also needed to become school governors and assist in the practical running and decision-making. School governors come from all walks of life and it's good to have a diverse mix, so nobody is excluded from applying. If your children are still at school, joining the PTA is a good move. You get to know the teachers personally which makes them more approachable – and more accessible should a problem occur. It also means that you find out about events at the planning stage – rather than two days after the event when you find a screwed up newsletter in a pocket when you're washing it!

You can also give your practical support to the school. Even if you don't have children at the school they will still be glad of some help and will value your contribution. Events need organisers, marshals, someone to make refreshments or take tickets at the door. And many hands make light work of clearing up afterwards. Fundraising is often a big issue in schools and PTA events provide much needed resources, which your children will directly benefit from.

All these events will bring you into contact with new people with a shared interest. You'll also get to know children your own are mixing with, and this will give you an insight into what makes your children tick. Maybe their friends will recognise you as a sympathetic ear and a sounding board when they struggle with teenage angst and their own parents "just don't understand". It's about widening your boundaries and enlarging your territory.

Some Christian organisations have excellent links with schools and regularly have opportunities for Christians to go in and chat with pupils. Volunteers are asked to go into classrooms for pre-arranged sessions to share their experience of being a Christian in their chosen field of work.

Visit www.scriptureunion.org.uk for further information.

'Children today are tyrants. They contradict their parents, gobble their food and tyrannise their teachers'
Socrates 469 – 399 BC

Mothers & Daughters

"My daughter and her classmates turned sixteen this year", writes Jo, "and the end of term is a disorganised affair, with the girls not really getting together again as a form after their exams are completed. I organised a 'Mothers and Daughters' event at a local restaurant, and held it in March, just before revision fever took hold.

I sent out an invitation stating clearly that the object of the meal was to say encouraging things about our daughters before their exams. I suggested there would be a prize for the most effusive and embarrassing mum! Thirty mothers and daughters responded and paid a deposit, so we were on! By the time the meal finished the restaurant was really noisy, so I commandeered a quieter part of the restaurant and we all moved upstairs.

I'd intended to go first, to encourage other mums to follow suit, but my one Christian friend got in first. We'd not had any prior discussion, and it was just marvellous to have her alongside. This fantastic lady was not only raising her own daughter, but for a year had also been looking after another school friend whose own family had returned to Germany. As she read a poem from the Mum in Germany the girls began to weep. Then she blessed her own daughter, and said how Jesus had made all the difference in their lives. So, now I'm ready to go second, but the next mum who pops up overtakes me. She's just had chemotherapy for breast cancer and is wearing a wig. It's very poignant, because we all know what a tough year this lovely family has had. Off she goes, singing the praises of her youngest daughter and blessing the socks off her. We're all sobbing now, because it's so real and not stage-managed in any way. Next comes a Jewish mum. Then another. I finally get my turn, but there's very little for me to say that the others haven't said.

Finally, one of the girls stood up. She had come without her mum and was clearly very moved. She was a Hindu. 'Since the moment we got upstairs, I have been feeling all trembly,' she said. 'I think this evening has been wonderful and I want to thank you very much for organising it.'

So that was that! The evening exceeded my wildest dreams. We've got three sons to get through before my final daughter sits her GCSE's, so the next evening should be 'Dads and Lads', but that's another story!"

An idea like this gives the opportunity for an annual reunion, allowing you to keep in touch with those you've made an initial contact with.

The **Spare** Bedroom

If you have a spare room in your house would you be willing to share it from time to time?

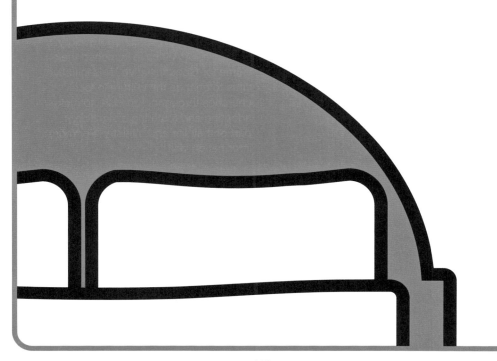

> '**And mighty proud I am, and ought to be thankful to God almighty,** that I am able to have a spare bed for my friends'
>
> **The Diary of Samuel Pepys**

Overseas Students

Overseas students are often not able to go home in the holidays because the cost of the airfare is prohibitive. This makes them vulnerable and lonely, particularly at Christmas, when the rest of Britain is clearly celebrating.

The organisation HOST can link you up with a lonely student who would be grateful to stay in a family home over the holidays. Small acts of kindness cost us very little and can enrich our lives and widen our own horizons, and they are appreciated so much by the recipients.
www.hosts-international.com

Fostering

Thousands of vulnerable children are in care in this country, desperately in need of loving homes. Every day more than 50 children are taken into care in the UK. They are removed from chaotic, traumatic, abusive, neglectful or desperate situations.

The Church is uniquely placed to offer its help to meet this need. As a large social network with involvement of large numbers of families, the Church is fertile soil for recruitment. Once carers have been through the full process of assessment, the Church could also provide an excellent community of support to wrap around families who are adopting or fostering children.

The Evangelical Alliance, along with Care for the Family, and The Churches' Child Protection Advisory Service (CCPAS) have launched their Home for Good initiative. This initiative aims to change the culture in local churches throughout the UK, to make adopting and fostering a significant part of their life and ministry. For more information visit www.eauk.org

There are lots of fostering agencies around the country that will be happy to chat informally about what's involved, or contact your local Social Services Fostering Department. More information at www.baaf.org.uk. The Christian writer and speaker Krish Kandiah is a strong advocate of fostering; he is fascinating to follow on Twitter (@krishk).

When an alien lives with you in your land, do not ill-treat him. **The alien living with you must be treated as one of your native born.** Love him as yourself, for you were aliens in Egypt. I am the Lord your God.
Leviticus 19:33-34

Tesol

Janet spent a week on an introductory TESOL course (Teaching English to Speakers of other Languages). It offered so many possibilities for getting alongside people and she found it so stimulating, that she went on to take the full five-week course.

She now helps in a unit in an inner city area where refugees and asylum seekers go to learn English. She finds it a privilege to get to know the students and to show love and patience, sitting alongside them week after week as they struggle with our alphabet, verbs, tenses and pronunciation. There are occasionally opportunities to say something specifically Christian but that's not the aim of the lessons. Janet says, 'There are more opportunities when we celebrate Christmas or Easter and can invite them to special events'.

Our university towns and cities have increasing numbers of overseas students keen to understand the British way of life, to visit our homes and to know what Christians believe. One student, who expressed a hope that she would make friends with English people and be invited into their homes, was told by her tutor that this was extremely unlikely, as English people didn't invite foreigners into their homes.

Janet and her husband have hosted a number of groups in their home where international students can come for supper and then study the Bible for an hour. Several students have asked to attend church with them, and some have become Christians. "I've felt as if God has been saying 'Janet, I'm working here. Would you like to come and join me?' What a privilege! Yes, the world is on my doorstep – and yours. This is God's world and he is at work in it."

Friends International is a helpful organisation for connecting Christians with overseas visitors an students. **www.friendsinternational.org.uk**

Refugees and Asylum Seekers

100 miles away, in another urban area, Jean was teaching English to Asian women when a variety of asylum seekers began attending her classes. She recognised that they all had in common a sense of shock, bereavement and isolation, and she began inviting them home for meals.

"One of the men seemed withdrawn, lacking in confidence and a bit scruffy and I assumed he was semi-literate. It took several weeks and some mutual hospitality to recognise that this man was intelligent, cultured and charming. He was an engineering graduate, spoke fluent Russian and two Afghan languages and had been brought up in a wealthy family.

I have learnt to see past first impressions. Most of the refugees I meet are highly intelligent with sophisticated political opinions and a sense of justice. I have also come to see that these are family men and women who have fled from death and who ache to see and hold their children, parents and wives. Their existence is lonely and confused. Often their sleep is tormented by nightmares. England is a cold and inhospitable place and we locals often fail to see the depth of their pain.

It's worth getting to know the asylum seekers in the local area. Their problems may almost overwhelm us but they value the genuine welcome that comes when we invite them into our homes for a meal. Several churches have now started drop-in sessions, befriending and offering practical help and hospitality. If there are asylum seekers housed in your community why not consider this as part of your outreach?"

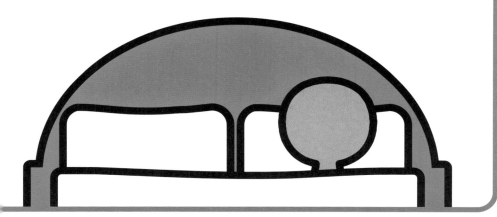

Knitting

With celebrities like Scarlett Johansson, Geri Halliwell, and Julia Roberts publicly declaring their devotion to the humble art of knit one, purl one, the recent success of knitting clubs shouldn't surprise us. With all the publicity about stress amongst women, knitting is seen as a great stress reliever; one devotee said 'you get into a kind of rhythm which I find relaxing.'

One London based knitting group feels knitting is a great icebreaker – it's not unusual to find artists, office workers and city professionals clicking side by side and the conversations which then ensue have all sorts of possibilities.

Teddies for Tragedy offer knitting patterns to make clothes which are then sent to children in war torn countries, where they have lost everything. There are various knitting patterns available; one is for a child's jumper, which needs very little sewing up and the other is for a small teddy that will be sent off in his own little drawstring bag. The knitted items are transported free of charge along with other shipments of humanitarian aid. Could you rally a group to knit Teddies for Tragedy or make small drawstring bags to send the teddies in?
www.teddiesfortragedies.org.uk

Craft

Crafts are making a comeback, so why not while away the winter nights with a small group who are knitting, quilting, stitching or making other forms of craft? You could buy each other's efforts for presents, or learn new skills from each other. There are numerous books available in the library – so there's no excuse for idle hands. The community website Pinterst (www.pinterest.com) is teeming with fanatistic ideas for crafts for all seasons and occasions covering all levels of ability.

'There is practically no activity that cannot be enhanced or replaced by knitting, if you really want to get obsessive about it.'
Stephanie Pearl McPhee

Pottery Painting

If you want to be a little more adventurous you could organise a group event with a difference and try your hand at designing plates and teapots. Pottery painting is a new craze. There are lots of Pottery Cafés where you can meet a group for tea and biscuits or throw a party. Everything is provided for your group to design purpose-made pots – paint, sponges, aprons and pottery.

Scrapbooking

Scrapbooking is a very simple idea which appeals to all ages with men, women, children from around six years of age, grandparents and those in residential homes and hospices enjoying this form of creativity. The photographs we take over the years are priceless but in reality are often left in a box and forgotten. Scrapbooking encourages us to make the most of the pictures we take, making a record of our story to pass on to our families and friends, recording the things that are important to us. It's a way of preserving the past, enriching the present and inspiring hope for the future.

Rebecca runs evening workshops and classes in her home, inviting people to come and try their own first page. If they want to continue they come back each month and new

relationships are built. One woman, receiving chemotherapy treatment herself has set up a group for others she met at the hospital, to help them produce something meaningful and lasting for their families.

The opportunities are numerous. Work colleagues, friends, neighbours, relatives, those who grieve, those who want to write a life journal and those who need some time out of a busy life, can all be reached. The conversations, which take place while the group is working on their pages, provide great opportunities to make new relationships.

Hobbies

Often the spare room is the place where raw materials are stored for hobbies. You might keep a sewing or knitting machine in there, or embroidery and tapestry yarns. You might keep glue and ribbons for card making or scrap-booking. Or your spare room might be the place you go to do jigsaws or build models.

With all these things you can choose to be solitary or inclusive. Do them alone, or as part of a small group. If you do share with others this gives lots of opportunities to share your perspective on life.

The Attic

The attic is often where we store our junk, or the stuff we only use occasionally. Sometimes the only time we head up here is to look for the Christmas decorations box.

Advent

This is traditionally a time at the beginning of the church year when the church is meant to examine itself. We pray about it and consider if we think we are where God wants us to be. So, as the body of Christ in your area, perhaps you could look at your individual and collective impact on the community.

As we make personal preparation for Christmas, how can we share this time and draw neighbours and friends in? The loft is probably the home for boxes of swags and baubles and other Christmas decorations. As you consider how you might celebrate Christmas, do think about those for whom this is the loneliest time of the year. Festivities seem to go on indefinitely if you're not a part of them

and, in the run-up to Christmas, the television is full of adverts depicting happy families. Christmas is one of the busiest times of year for The Samaritans, as people are most acutely aware of their loneliness and isolation. Over thirty percent of households in Britain now comprise of one person, many of whom have no close family or friends to celebrate with.

Christmas is a perfect time for getting people together. Can you have an open house this Christmas and invite lonely neighbours and acquaintances to share food? Don't feel you have to supply it all, people prefer to contribute. If you've got people from other countries living locally why not ask them to bring some traditional food from their homeland? You'll be amazed at how enriched your celebrations will be and the novelty and informality takes away all the pressure of everything having to be just right.

Even the food preparation can be a great community thing. Peeling carrots and shelling peas together is a good way to relax and get to know each other. By the time the food is ready to eat the ice will be well and truly broken. Tell stories, maybe get everyone to share childhood Christmas memories, good or bad, and ask what they would most like to have in their stocking this year.

Washing up can be communal too. Don't feel you must do it all. You're providing the meeting place and the invitations. People like to help so be gracious and let them. That way you'll be more willing to do it again, and others might feel they can reciprocate if you don't set such an impossible standard that they're afraid they can't match.

Tearfund produce Christmas resource packs (visit the Tearfund website at **www.tearfund.org**).

Easter

Why not consider some Easter activities with friends? For all your chocoholic friends why not organise a chocolate party? Alternatively, you could do Easter crafts, or arrange an egg rolling and Easter egg hunt for families.

Lent

February brings another opportunity for bringing out what you've got in the house. Shrove Tuesday is traditionally the time for using up all your store-cupboard perishables before the Lenten fast begins.

Why not throw a Pancake Party for your neighbours and friends? You'll need plenty of milk and some eggs and flour, but consider asking each person to bring an unusual filling, enough for everyone to sample.

New Year

Each year begins with the opportunity to make New Year's Resolutions.

Our challenge to you, whatever time of year you read this, is to attempt to come alongside at least one new person this year, so that you can: bless them, spend time with them, meet their needs and then proclaim the gospel to them (Luke 10). 'Each One Reach One' is the resolution we are asking you to consider.

Write it on a post-it note and stick it by your telephone.

The Granny Flat

Retirement

People view retirement in a variety of ways – for some it is a longed-for freedom, for others it is impending doom carrying the threat of boredom, inertia and a feeling of being on the scrap heap. For many people there is a real fear of ageing.

The 4 stages of life are usually categorised as follows:

1st Age: dependence, socialization, immaturity, education (childhood)

2nd Age: independence, maturity, responsibility (possibly raising children), earning

3rd Age: personal fulfillment, active independence

4th Age: dependence and dignity.

There are currently around 12 million British people in the 3rd & 4th ages. This is a great mission field. Older people are now finding a new freedom as they retire from work and look for new pastimes – things they really want to do now they are free from obligations and demands of employment and bringing up children. Many use their time creatively and find new skills in painting or other crafts. Others take advantage of low season holidays or preferential rates at leisure facilities. And for those who prefer to flex their intellectual muscles there are courses available with the University of the Third Age.

No need to rush off to work or worry about the potentially negative impact on your career. Our increased longevity has given us a completely new map of life – but often the focus is on the problem of ageing while the enormous potential of the third age is not always recognised.

Those over sixty possess both competence and availability, a precious combination, especially in relation to Christian ministry. It can be a great time for making new friends, getting to know your neighbours and sharing your faith with others in a relaxed way. It can be the best time of your life, as in Robert's Browning's poem 'Grow old along with me, the best is yet to be'.

Many people who share this sentiment are taking opportunities for early retirement. Sports personalities are forced to retire early, which is great if you've earned enough in a short career to be comfortable

'Don't simply retire from something: have something to retire to.'

Harry Emerson Fosdick

throughout your life, even better if you've been particularly successful in your chosen field. Muhammad Ali famously said on announcing his retirement: "I want to get out with my greatness intact."

While modesty prevents most of us from agreeing with Ali's comment, there is something to be said for quitting while you're ahead. Some retired people take on the responsibility for looking after grandchildren while their parents are at work. Again this gives lots of opportunity to get alongside others and share our faith. Relationships can be struck at the school gate, toddler groups, and swimming or dancing lessons. As we bring our collective experience into parenting groups it's a good way of brushing up on 'rusty' parenting skills.

Do you have a 'Caleb' attitude to retirement? He couldn't wait to get to the promised land. He'd caught a glimpse of this highland paradise on earth while on a preliminary survey forty-five years previously and then,

at last he was about to go in and enjoy its delights despite being 85 years old.

It can be easy to slip into the attitude of 'leaving it to the younger ones' yet there are so many opportunities to make a difference whatever our age.

Doris's story

Doris was 74 years old and lived in sheltered accommodation. She had invited her neighbours to church events but they were not interested; she had little money and felt that she couldn't do anything useful for God. Doris spent much of her time knitting and often sat alone at home engaged in this craft. It seems, so are some of her neighbours. Doris saw the potential for making real friendships with the other residents by inviting them for afternoon tea each week, and spending the time knitting together. This soon became their favourite afternoon of the week, and they shared many knitting projects together as well as getting to know each other.

Hazel's story

As a fifteen year old, recuperating from an illness, Hazel felt God's call to the mountainous regions of China. Forty years later she had the chance to 'spy out the land' when she completed a 100km sponsored walk along the Great Wall of China in 1999 for the Children's Society. She subsequently joined a short term team working in an orphanage in China in 2002 and since then has spent several months in China using her skills as a paediatric physiotherapist.

More recently she's spent six weeks in Morocco setting up day centres for children with physical handicaps. Her accounts of her travels and the ways God is using her are inspiring, challenging and at times quite scary, yet she loves it all, and is making a real difference.

Liza's story

Fiona Castle's older sister, Liza, at the age of 73, sold her home, left her friends and moved to inner city Manchester to work on the Eden Project. This is her story. 'When my husband died seven years ago, I looked at my life and said to the Lord, "Lord, I am tired of the comfort zone, I want to be at the 'coal face'. I am willing to sell up and move into the slums of Manchester, Liverpool, London or wherever, but I must hear from you exactly the place of your choosing.

I was assigned to Eden Harpurhey, a difficult district two and a half miles from the centre of Manchester. Intercessors had been praying for 18 years for Christians to move into Harpurhey. Samantha came to an Alpha course I was asked to lead, an alcoholic for many years with seven children living in a back-to-back two-bedroom house. On that first day she wanted to be different and invited Jesus into her life to change it. Going through exhausting withdrawal symptoms, prayer was given, asking God to enable her to become an overcomer.

The response quickly came, "No, we need Grannies and Mums!"

"That time came in the summer of 2002. I heard a talk by Andy Hawthorne from the 'Message Trust', a Christian outreach to young people in the deprived areas of Manchester, who were running wild on the streets learning to become 'prison fodder'. As Andy spoke all my 'spiritual bells' began to ring, and when he called for volunteers, willing to give up at least seven years of their lives to live and work in those difficult areas, I wondered if this was what I was waiting for.

Eventually I rang The Message and asked, "Am I too old at 73 to come and join one of your Eden teams?" The response quickly came, "No, we need Grannies and Mums!"

From that moment she was healed of her alcoholism. Such was the change in her that family and friends wanted to know about 'this Christianity.' Samantha was discipled well by her Christian neighbour and began to give her family strong loving boundaries. Consequently the children became quieter and happier. The youngest changed so much, his teachers were asking what had transformed him so dramatically. Samantha now holds meetings regularly in her home where family and friends can ask questions and learn about Jesus. The wonderful harvest from this one seed, sown in the ground with love and prayers, continues to grow and spread."

The **Conservatory**

The Conservatory is often the room where we can sit, reflect and take stock of our lives. Take a quiet few minutes to look at your own life by considering the questions below.

Imagine that one day, long after you have passed away, one of your great-grandchildren asks about you and your life. How would you want to be remembered and described?
Write a summary of your life, as you would like it to be related to your great-grandchild. Be sure to include a description of your values and your personal characteristics. Put this to one side for a couple of days and then come back to it. Think not only about what you included in your summary but also what you left out.

Are there activities that take up a great deal of your time that weren't included? Why did you leave them out? What changes could you make in your life so that the summary would be an accurate picture of your life?

Sharing the responses to these questions with others in a group could be helpful to everyone. It's the sort of exercise a life coach might recommend, to help someone wanting to move on in their lives.

We've already seen that people today are actively searching for a meaning to life and this is one reason why they are reading an increasing number of self-help books and flocking to life coaches to help them sort out their lives and fulfil their potential. Years ago they may have looked for advice from their local church, but now run miles from anything which might be Christian. This might be because many Christians can hear hundreds of sermons, Sunday after Sunday yet still have no real idea of how to relate what they hear on a Sunday to their everyday lives during the rest of the week.

The increasing popularity of self help books emphasise the interest many people having in improving their lifestyles.

Laurie Beth-Jones, an American author, has written a book called, 'Jesus, Life Coach' which lays out a faith based programme to help get our lives in shape, with Jesus as our personal trainer.

The book suggests that we all want to be led by someone who will save us time, give us new ideas, connect with us on a personal level and stay with us on the journey, and Jesus promises all this, and more. The questions at the end of each chapter offer the opportunity for any group to enjoy some stimulating discussion while looking at important principles for life, like focus, balance, productivity and fulfilment.

A look at the New Testament shows us that Jesus was the master life coach. People flocked to him. He constantly affirmed them, adjusted to them and inspired them. His coming to earth was the greatest single act of rapport building in the world. We can't read The Great Commission without realising that Jesus gave people clear goals, a map to follow with Himself beside. It's ironic that Jesus often comes up in secular life coaching as a model to follow.

Storytelling

Some people might have been quite put off their Coco Pops one morning by a grim article in The Daily Telegraph which revealed the sad fact that the sweet nursery rhymes we chanted in the playground were not quite the innocent little ditties they appeared to be. In fact they had their origins in rather sordid adult rhymes, which our illiterate ancestors sang to lull their children to sleep because they didn't actually know any others.

Fortunately our children will not be quite as bereaved as we are by these revelations, because they had long ago abandoned our tame little skipping chants and wimpy Fairy Tales in favour of the more gutsy versions entitled 'Revolting Rhymes' written in the 1980's by Roald Dahl. Try reading them for a lesson in cultural relevance if ever there was one! But, even allowing for modern interpretations like this, we have a history of storytelling, which goes back to the beginning of time. Stories were passed down the generations and created a rich heritage.

Everyone loves a story. "The most fun weekend I've had in ages" was one woman's description of the two-day story-telling course she attended. "You go to play, to tell stories, to analyse what they mean and why they're interesting." On her course the mix was 50:50 male to female with most in their 30s and 40s and lively!

There is something special about the tradition of sitting around the fireside and telling stories while your audience looks you in the eye. It seems that the ancient art of storytelling has been enjoying a revival in recent years, with schools, libraries and hospitals all using story-tellers. Why not launch a story-telling group in your community?

One group in Scotland did just that, aimed particularly at children in the school holidays. Carol writes:

"When I was growing up it was still common for extended families to live close together. Children could spend time with parents, grandparents, aunts and uncles and hear all manner of stories, many told without books. I recall learning many of the classic fairy stories, fantasies that included my favourite toys, animals and people, basic Bible stories and characters and my family's history in this way. It appeared to me that telling stories from memory, from the heart like this, seemed to come so naturally to that generation.

Now, as life gets busier and more frantic for all of us, it's not easy for many parents to find the time, let alone the inclination or inspiration to fulfil this role. So we decided to hold a storytelling event – something traditional and relaxing – bringing together a few of the most harassed members of the community to experience quality time with family and friends. We put up posters and contacted friends to ask for their support.

Having received little response from our adverts we were thrilled as the room started to fill with children and their mums or minders. Our story-teller, Grace, immediately put them at ease and the children and adults were spellbound, relaxed and happy as Grace gently and thoughtfully carried us through the Creation story layer by layer, using balloons, fabrics, stuffed animals and other carefully chosen props. All too soon time came to share in refreshments and chat. As we said our goodbyes, the reluctance of our guests to leave assured us we had made new friends and opened a fresh door to some people."

Jesus was a master storyteller with a perfect knack for getting his message across by using all surrounding things to illustrate his point. We need to learn from him how to communicate effectively and speak into people's lives convincingly.

In his book 'Faith in a Changing Culture', John Drane outlines the importance of storytelling. He starts by introducing God's story. He's active and present in our world and we should tell these stories about him. As the book says,

The Bible unhesitatingly affirms that God is constantly at work in the world in many ways, times and places. Evangelism is not about Christians working on God's behalf because God is powerless without them. Effective evangelism must start with recognising where God is already at work, and getting alongside God in what is going on there. God's story, not ours, is the authentic starting point.

So, let's go out and tell the greatest story ever told.

The Garden

Barbecues & Picnics

Summer is traditionally the time for barbecues – lots of sizzling sausages and burgers. But perhaps it's time for a new, healthy approach. There have been many articles warning us of obesity in the press recently. Remember the Galloping Gourmet? Well, he's now a Christian as well as a passionate advocate for healthy eating. He says this, "How many people died on 9/11? I think it was 2,843. In the US this year 100 times that number will die from overeating. The UK is behind but on a similar curve." So, whilst eating out will always be a popular pastime, why not offer your neighbours and friends a healthier option – less food but better quality? Barbecue good lean meat with lightweight sauces, lots of salad and baked potatoes. Advertise it as being 'good for the heart.' Perhaps even use it as a fundraiser to send money to a heart disease charity.

'Gardens and flowers have a way of bringing people together, drawing them from their homes'

Helen of Troy

Bonfire Party

Many of us have fond childhood memories of the towering pyre on the waste ground on the corner, on which everyone piled the rubbish from their attic.

Then, as the flames began to lick around an old settee, the acrid smoke would sting our eyes and cause everyone to scatter into the shadows. Sparks might well fly if you attempted this now – certainly environmental health would be affected. But there's something about a fire that draws people to gather.

Why not gather a group yourself? If you can't manage a mini bonfire you could invest in a chiminea from the garden centre and have a mini log fire in the garden. Appease traditionalists with some homemade treacle toffee, baked potatoes, mulled wine and 'lashings of ginger beer'. People often feel far more involved in an event if they can contribute to it in some way. Suggest each person or family brings a box of fireworks (cost to be agreed beforehand) and something towards the food.

People often feel far more involved in an event if they can contribute to it in some way. There's no need to go overboard with fireworks and please do ensure local health and safety regulations are adhered to.

If you're really brave you could give all the little ones a sparkler and get them to write their name in the air. Then tell them (loud enough for their parents to hear) that Jesus already knows their name – he has it written on his heart. Pray for a starry night and you'll have even more opportunity to point out the glory of God. "The heavens declare the glory of God; the skies proclaim the work of his hands." Psalm 19:1.

Events like this, prior to Christmas may make it easier to invite people to something special at Christmas at which they'll have the opportunity to hear about the real reason for the season.

Days out with a Difference

Jane was brought up in isolation in the wilds of west Wales and became aware of God through what he has made. She learnt to read God's presence in the wide-open sky, majestic cliffs and the loneliness of the desolate warrens. She wondered how tired, stressed out twenty-first-century people would react to being made aware of the wonder of God's creation.

Jesus used the physical world as a starting point for some of his teaching

and used birds, flowers and the sky as visual aids (Luke 12:7,27,54), so why not do the same?
Jane organised a day consisting of a waterfall walk and a meal in a local hotel followed by an illustrated talk along the lines of the special interest events advertised in 'What's on this weekend' newspaper columns.

Bouncy Castles

If you thought Bouncy Castles were just for children, think again. Some hire companies are now renting them to adults and throwing in some boxing gloves. Great for parties and an opportunity to prove that Christians are not wimps! Ring around the hire companies in your area for competitive prices. Some firms provide blow-up clubs to batter your opponent off Gladiator-style pedestals. Fun for all ages, and great for breaking the ice in your community. It could add a new dimension to a traditional barbecue.

Garden Parties / Open Gardens

Perhaps you would consider organising an event based on gardening hints – like a local Gardener's World, or arrange a hanging basket demonstration. This could be held at your local garden centre if you don't feel you can do it yourself.

If your garden is a large one you might consider opening it to the public. Alternatively, a group of people with more modest gardens can plan a tour. Be ready to answer questions about plants and flowers. You might be able to sell seeds and cuttings or arrange plant swaps. Take a look at www.quietgarden.org for other ways of using your garden.

Outdoor Films

An outdoor film night is a great success, though you'll need to wait until dusk for the picture to be clear enough. You can project the film onto your house wall or a screen using a projector that you hopefully will be able to borrow from your local school or church. Make sure everyone brings a comfortable chair and is equipped for a drop in temperature. Use Citronella candles to deter midges and pass around crisps and popcorn.

Camping

One group wanted to concentrate on building strong links with whole families and camping seemed a good way to include everyone. Camp was set up in the large garden of one home by the mums and children and the local Guides lent their dining and loo tents.

Everyone arrived by 6.30pm for a barbecue and communal games followed. A walk through local fields and woods began at 8pm and the torchlight gave it all a magical feel. Hot chocolate, singing and stories around a bonfire followed before the children fell into their beds exhausted. The adults returned to the fire and particularly the men started to get to know each other and began to have some 'real' conversations. In the morning there were cereals and bacon butties, and more games before camp was packed up by midday.

The event was followed with regular get togethers for Sunday lunch and walks and everyone is keen to repeat the camp next summer, but it will probably be twice the size. The secret of its success was the prayer for individuals beforehand.

The Garage

Everyone thinks they need a house with a garage in order to put the car away. But the majority of us end up not being able to fit the car in because of all the things we store in our garages.

How about a de-clutter session and then taking a stall at a local car boot sale? You'll be amazed at the people you meet and chat to. One enterprising group set up a stall offering free food if people took a leaflet with some challenging faith questions.

Take a look at the things you have stored in your garage and consider how they might help others. Do you have tools that are redundant that could be sent to a third world country to help them with farming? Two men in Ireland set up a charity for shipping hand tools abroad and they are always looking for more old hand tools and if you have any you don't use any more email tools.belfast@virgin.net

And what about your car? When you have it serviced or have the tyres checked do you ever chat with the people doing it? At the very least you can leave a relevant leaflet in the car so that the mechanic can glance at it; it might just speak right into their life.

Here's Jenny's Story

'Our local garage is wonderful. Three brothers run it and they're very personable and chat about their families and they fall over themselves to give a brilliant service. One of my friends lives right near there. She called them out to start her car several times and they refused money but told her they liked chocolate biscuits. So I occasionally drop in with a box of biscuits and a card telling them how much I appreciate them. (I do the same with the car spares shop who insist on fitting bulbs and wiper blades for me – I must have perfected the pathetic woman look!)

Perhaps I shouldn't admit this in print, but recently I forgot to book in for my MOT and realized with horror that it had expired a few weeks earlier. The garage fitted me in the same day. When I went to pick it up I commented on the Rogues Gallery page in our local press, which listed the sins of locals who have been in trouble. Some listings are for driving without documentation and I could well have featured among them! The mechanic grinned at me and said, "God looks after his own." So I told him that was true in so many ways and if he believed that, he'd better join God's gang straight away.

Another time I went to get my tyres checked at another local supplier. He was looking for my toolkit and opened my boot, which is stacked high with evangelism resources. He turned and grinned at me and asked, "Are you leaving home?" When I said this was work stuff he asked, "Well, what kind of a vicar are you?"

I told him I wanted to connect faith with modern culture and he asked me if anyone had ever talked to me about out of body experiences. With a bit of prompting he told me about his own experience of this phenomenon. He acknowledged that the essence, which was him, was able to exist separately from the shell, which is his body. I asked him if he was able to accept that when his body died this would be able to continue to exist and he agreed. So I asked him "Where do you want it to go?"

That was obviously a powerful question and he reacted, "Wow, are you asking me do I want it to live in heaven or Hawaii?"

When I nodded he said he needed time to think about that one. So I told him that was fine but pointed out that only God knew him intimately and loved him unconditionally. Only God was able to heal his brokenness and make him whole and happy. I've left him to think about it. My customer details are on the computer and we've chatted about my church so he knows where to find me in an emergency. Otherwise I'm leaving it to God to prompt him to follow up the conversation next time I get my tyre treads checked.

There are so many God-given opportunities to talk about our faith. We can't always expect to give the same three point message, sometimes people will approach us from random angles, and we just need to be able to identify a potential peg on which we can hang our message.

Shoeboxes

How many shoes boxes are you hanging onto just in case something goes wrong with the shoes and you need to return them? Can they be filled with gifts for an underprivileged child? Samaritan's Purse is one of several organisations that send lorry-loads of shoeboxes to war-torn countries every year. Operation Christmas Child brings joy and hope to children in desperate situations around the world through gift-filled shoeboxes and the good news of God's love.

This programme of Samaritan's Purse provides an opportunity for people of all ages to be involved in a simple, hands-on mission project while focusing on the true meaning of Christmas, Jesus Christ, God's greatest gift. Along with shoebox gifts, millions of children are given gospel booklets in their own language. They collect over 6.6 million shoebox gifts worldwide and distribute them to children in some 95 countries.

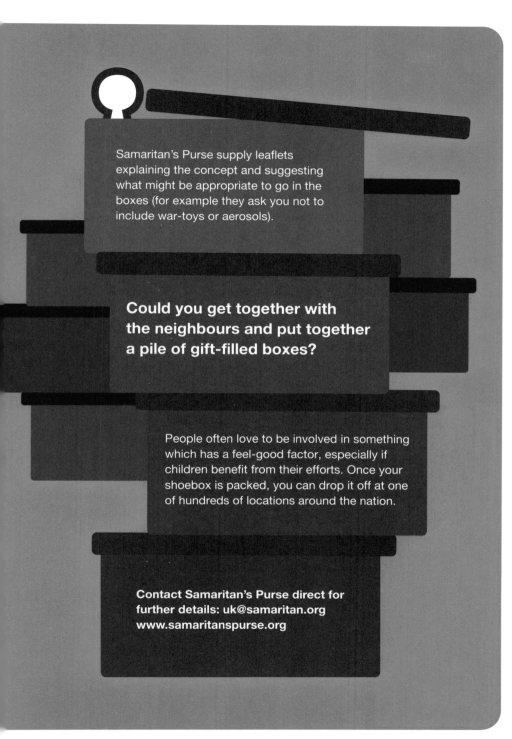

Samaritan's Purse supply leaflets explaining the concept and suggesting what might be appropriate to go in the boxes (for example they ask you not to include war-toys or aerosols).

Could you get together with the neighbours and put together a pile of gift-filled boxes?

People often love to be involved in something which has a feel-good factor, especially if children benefit from their efforts. Once your shoebox is packed, you can drop it off at one of hundreds of locations around the nation.

Contact Samaritan's Purse direct for further details: uk@samaritan.org www.samaritanspurse.org

Outside

Ideas themed inside a house are generally small and within your comfort zone. Sometimes God might call you and enable you to step right outside and start doing something completely different...

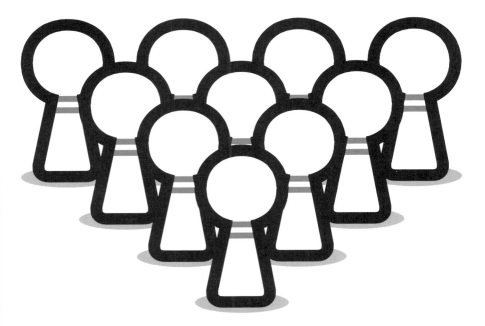

Sport

For many people, joining their local running, football, swimming or tennis club can be a great way of meeting new people and building up relationships with them. Think of a sport you've always wanted to develop your skills in and find out what's already available in your area, and join in. Sometimes it's more effective to become involved in something already organised, than to start something new.

your door

International Evening

"What are we going to do next?" was the question on the lips of the group responsible for coordinating events at a N.W. London church. Sue reports on the answer. 'One look at the 100 plus congregation, consisting of people from approximately 25-30 different countries and we had the answer. An International Evening! What better way to celebrate the diversity of our environment than to offer the opportunity to invite their friends, family and colleagues to a fun evening.

We publicised the evening using brightly coloured invitation cards decorated with flags and awaited the arrival of the guests, many wearing their national costume or international clothes they have acquired at some point, but never had the opportunity to wear! By prior arrangement, they brought some of the most delicious food you have ever tasted – yes, it really is curried goat over there!

On arrival everyone was given a glass of fruit punch and encouraged to take part in an icebreaker quiz, such as identifying famous places or famous international personalities from photos placed around the room.

Later everyone moved into the main hall, colourfully decorated with flags and memorabilia from all over the world, where the food was labelled and arranged in various areas, representing different corners of the world e.g. African, Asian/Chinese, West Indian main courses, European salads, American desserts. Lots of informal recipe swapping ensued, as people tucked in and told each other how they cooked their particular dish.

Following the meal, there was a short talk, and then guests chose to go and watch a variety of demonstrations on offer, from Chinese, Russian and West Indian cooking, Indian sari dressing, African hair-braiding, African head wraps and tie-dyeing. These sessions have proved to be extremely interesting and entertaining. Coffee and mints were then served and people stayed to chat long into the evening with new friends'.

151

Katie's Story

Having moved to a new area, Katie found it easy to get to know lots of other Christian couples and families. But she was aware that she didn't have many friends outside of church. She had always loved playing netball at school and when she mentioned this, someone at church suggested they set up a church netball night. Instead, she felt called to join a team that was already operating locally and committed to playing every Thursday evening. The netball was fast and furious with injuries and very competitive matches. Often there was the chance to head to the local pub for a drink afterwards and conversation flowed freely.

Keeping Thursdays free for netball was quite a commitment and often church meetings would clash, but Katie continued to enjoy her matches and tried very hard to never miss a week. Strong bonds of friendship grew and the 'netball girls' supported each other through more than matches.

Christians in Sport have a variety of resources and run one, five and nine day courses to help Christians use sporting activities to share God's love. Take a look at their website for more ideas and information –
www.christiansinsport.org.uk

Fit Lives

Going out with a keep-fit programme means you widen your horizons while narrowing your waistline. Join a gym, running club or keep fit class, sign up at weight-watchers, and visit the health spa. Invite some neighbours to come with you. Often people fancy going but don't want to go alone. Toning up is much more fun with company and you'll make new friends as well as facing the world as a fitter, healthier specimen!

Often people go to the gym to meet others. In numerous surveys people stated that they joined a gym to make friends, yet they left because they find that they have used the gym without a single person speaking to them. It seems, then, that this would be a perfect opportunity to befriend others and if you love going to the gym why not see this as an opportunity to share God's love in that environment?

Susannah Pilkington is the executive officer for Fit Lives, a small charitable trust, committed to bring the love of Christ to people through fitness venues and activities. "I used to think evangelism was something scary, to be avoided. I thought it included a soapbox on a street corner, or door knocking and interrupting people eating their tea – aarrgghh!"

Susannah grins. "Then the penny dropped and I realised that God wanted me to work for him by doing exactly what I enjoyed – down at the gym. It was a huge release and I suddenly understood what Jesus meant by, "My yoke is easy and my burden is light."

Fit Lives want to recruit co-ordinators who are comfortable in a health club environment and are willing to provide personal support to members and staff. Activities undertaken depend on the skill and fitness of the co-ordinator. Their main task is to provide a friendly face to staff and users of the club, because Fit Lives believe that offering a listening ear in a time-poor society is really valuable and demonstrates care.

The organisation sets up and runs a small library in each club. They aim to run occasional lifestyle seminars and video-based courses, offering a Christian perspective to relevant issues such as image, self-worth, time management, business ethics, marriage, and parenting.

They also offer Alpha courses which have proved highly successful, with people saying they would never have gone to their local church to attend the course, but as it was held in their club they felt they could 'give it a go'.

Some Health Clubs offer dry cleaning, travel agency services, a take-away food service and video libraries. It's not difficult to offer a special deal to encourage people to join. The problem is getting them to stay and, in an attempt to do this, the clubs are striving to meet people's physical, social and spiritual needs. In short, they are trying to create a community where people feel they belong. It's easy to leave an establishment, much harder to leave a group of people.

Perhaps our churches have something to learn here!

Realising that relationships are the key, the clubs are often very welcoming to Christians who offer to visit regularly and assist them in this process. They know it makes good business sense! Some health clubs are so appreciative that they run an occasional fundraising event to assist with the work.

If you enjoy a particular sport, love the sauna or just feel at ease in the club coffee bar environment, then the chances are that you already have a head start by knowing people in your local club. So why not contact Fit Lives to ask about training as a Co-ordinator? No need to be super-fit or really sporty, the qualities required are social and communication skills combined with a heart for others and the backing of your church. The time commitment in each club is 8 hours a week. Take a look at the website www.fitlives.co.uk or contact Susannah Pilkington direct on: admin@fitlives.co.uk

Reach a Street

Reach-a-Street has become a way of life for the team who visit the same 25 houses each week, not a method or a project. It's not a way of getting people into the church but a way of serving and blessing people through the demonstration of faith. The purpose is to offer three jobs: gardening, taking items to the tip and car washing. With the same adult Christian leading the team, they can help take the inevitable opportunities to share their faith and offer prayer where appropriate. As time goes on and the relationships develop the team can become almost a counselling service, maybe run personal errands or meet any number of needs for the residents.

'We started reaching out this way after many years of feeling like salesmen when doing evangelism', says David, the team leader.

'Through a series of events we got to know a pastor from the Dream Center, Los Angeles. We were so convicted by the way they were seeing lives changed that we decided to visit them. We saw a ministry called Adopt-a-Block. Teams of people were literally adopting blocks of houses and giving their lives for them in practical, relational and spiritual ways. It just seemed we had found what we were looking for - a way of really loving people. We felt we could adapt this to the British way of life in a way that felt natural to us.

Society is changing. It is transient which means many do not even know their neighbours. Trust is diminishing rapidly causing many to feel self-sufficient. Reach-a-Street members come humbly into this situation offering trust, local friendships and stability. Surprisingly, we find nearly all the residents open to offers of help, prayer and friendship –

Quad Biking and Zorbing

Both of these activites have attracted a lot of attention in recent years and are great fun! Outdoor activity centres have set up downhill and cross country tracks that you can zoom round in muddy overalls or tumble down in a large plastic hamster ball, with or without beans! Cost can be prohibitive, so go for a quiet time of year and do some negotiating with the manager. Perhaps you could do a deal where different groups from your church or community can get a block discount? You take your group, then the youth department will go in a month and the men's outreach group will go the month after that. Most prices are up for negotiation. Be prepared for a lot of screaming and for some surprises as your quiet friend might be the one driving the fastest and taking the most risks through the deepest muddy puddles.

they kind of feel this is what the church should really be doing.

"How are you today, Simon?" I asked. "Not very well. My wife died in hospital and was buried yesterday." I was stunned. Within minutes we were crying and praying together. Simon's world had slowly fallen apart over the years. After the 'high' of his son winning a silver medal in the Olympics to the 'low' of his later suicide, this widower lives in a one-bedroom maisonette with his other son, who has severe learning difficulties. He can't bear to go back to his overgrown home where the suicide took place.

Reach a Street is built on the foundations of love and faithfulness. The world does not expect us to be unconditional towards them as they may have an alternate lifestyle or different beliefs. They are surprised that we are faithful, with some initially expecting us to fizzle out after a few months. But how else can we convince them of God's unconditional love, of a faithful, covenant love that never fails?

We have had our own spiritual lives deepened dramatically throughout the last five years whilst doing Reach-a-Street. We are discovering that getting close to people means getting close to God. Our hearts have been tested and our faith has been stretched as we are faced with people who are different to us and need miracles.'

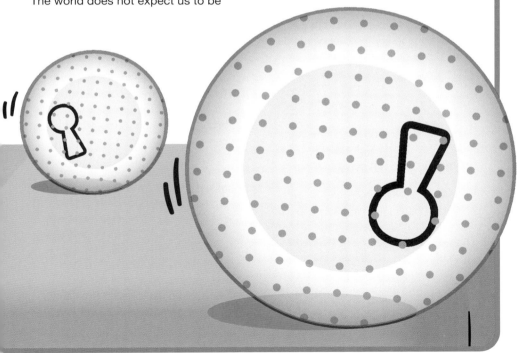

Johnny's Story

About a year ago my friend Connor was in an odd mood. One Sunday morning at our church in Ipswich, instead of looking up at the front singing the worship songs like everyone else, he spent most of the service staring outside. Although at the time we wondered what on earth was wrong with him, it turned out that he was counting. That Sunday Connor counted over 100 people walk past the church doors.

Next week, he took a table and set up a stand, after receiving a call at 9am that Sunday (disturbing my much

We even had communion a few times with those who wanted to take it. So, while 250 people were singing inside the building there was a church forming on the doorstep!

What had happened was Connor decided that people didn't need a sermon, they needed a chat, a friend and relationship. From these beginnings there grew what could only be described as a very, very odd family. In that 6 months we saw magnificent prayers of healing answered for our new friends and awesome friendships built. We had incredible conversations, and the privilege of standing alongside 20

"Wow, the spirit's really evident this morning, isn't it?"

loved Sunday morning lie in) myself and Connor were outside with two canisters of tea and coffee offering a free cup to anyone who walked past. The first two weeks it was just the two of us perhaps giving half a dozen cups out to the 150 or so who walked past.

However, after a month something happened. A few well known homeless men not only turned up specifically for a hot drink and biscuit, but they stayed, talked and shared. Three months later we had a base of about 20 to 30 people (many of them homeless, alcoholic, drug addicts and anti-religious) all drinking coffee, sharing a meal, sharing life and most weeks happy to talk about Jesus, no matter whether it was rain or shine.

homeless men sitting on the floor below the lectern cheering as one of our friends got baptised.

I headed off to college and had missed seeing my 'church friends' and was delighted to recognize Josh in the park, four months later. Josh had started his friendship with me at the coffee stand by saying "I'm not religious so don't try and convert me". On that sunny morning I opened the discussion by saying "Wow, the spirit's really evident this morning, isn't it?" I wasn't expecting much of a response but I am happy to say that his face lit up. "Isn't it amazing, did you hear? I'm on a membership course with Pete and Josh, we're getting baptized".

Community Prayer

At an event in Devon, a woman told how prayer was transforming her area. The streets around the church are divided up and each is visited on a regular basis, usually three monthly. During week one, the team visits each home in the street and explains that the following week the road will be the focus of prayer. Does the household have anything they'd like the church to pray for? Rarely is the door slammed in the faces of the team, as the residents are invariably facing some crisis from illness to redundancy.

When the team returns three months later, there are always answers to prayer, which occurred during the week that particular road was being prayed for. And the group have found that being willing to pray for a road means that at times they need to put feet on their prayers and become more involved with some of the families.

Unexpected

Kerry's Story

Some long-standing musician friends came over to visit from Ireland. They wanted to see lots of friends and knew it wasn't possible to get around everyone, so Pete - another of their friends - set up a Sunday lunchtime music session in a pub quite near to where we live and we went to join in. We don't tend to go in pubs very often as we get caught up so much with church events. I'm sure there is a lesson to be learned there!

Anyway, the session was a great success and lots of people gathered to hear the songs. The atmosphere was really friendly and people joined in and sang along. The landlady of the pub even brought drinks across to those who were leading the music.

I got chatting to Pete's girlfriend Marie and really liked her. During the course of the conversation I mentioned that we'd come straight from church and she seemed to ignore the comment totally and changed the subject, so I assumed she wasn't interested or might even be a bit hostile to Christianity.

The next time the Irish friends came over, Pete organised another session at the same pub, this time on the Sunday night and we went enthusiastically to join in. Marie had brought a neighbour along who'd been recently widowed and it turned out that our Vicar had conducted the funeral and they'd really liked him.

Marie then started talking to me about her own father's death. The family had nursed him for a long time, yet she said she still felt guilty about things. "For example – I regret that it didn't occur to me to say Night Prayers with him," she told me, "He always did them with us when we were little and I still say them regularly now. We ought to have done it together; I think it would have blessed him."

"Oh," I said, showing my surprise. "I didn't realise you were a believer," She assured me that she was and added that she'd been brought up as a Roman Catholic. We then talked about the importance of 'owning' the faith that you've been brought up with and I realised that she had indeed owned it. Though she wasn't part of a worshipping community, she talked to God when out riding or walking her dogs. It's just too easy to think that churchgoers have the monopoly on faith. I won't make that mistake again.

Encounters

Mandy's Story

I was late for work so the school drop off had to be a fast one! As I rushed past the school office the school secretary called out to me. She was looking a little out of her depth because a new mum, who had recently moved into the area, was in her office in tears. 'Perhaps you have time for a coffee with Mrs J this morning?' she said with pleading eyes. I did briefly think about how late I already was for work, then realised that I couldn't really ignore them and walk past. So Mrs J and I moved into the school parents' coffee lounge and I made her a rather weak cappuccino.

She dried her tears as she explained the hassles and heartaches of moving in to a new place, being lost and not knowing anyone. I didn't have many words of wisdom but was happy to listen and compare notes about my moves from the past. We exchanged mobile numbers and I walked her to her car, before heading off in a hurry to work.

A couple of texts later I mentioned to her that I was about to host a 'Christianity Explored' group in my house. The other mums I had asked were all good friends who I had built up relationships with over years. But Mrs J did say that she wanted to meet more mums, so I felt there was nothing to lose. The text came back two days later, saying that she didn't feel she was religious but that she would like to just get out of her house once a week and meet people.

She came and was delightful! Very open, happy to ask deep questions, genuinely interested in other people and their views and with a great sense of humour. She added so much to our little group and talked about how she felt closer to God by the end. When we tentatively suggested a follow on 'Discipleship Explored' Group she was the first to say yes. She was again the most regular attendee and has talked about coming along to try out church. I enjoy my conversations and friendship with her, and often think how close I came to rushing past and missing the unexpected encounter that God had planned for us both that morning.

> Unexpected encounters can often surprise us when we realise that God can use these as much as those we consider to be more significant conversations. The stories here are included to challenge and encourage you.

No Regrets

Stephen's Story

Tim was young, fit and healthy and always had a positive friendly manner. He helped me out in the garden every week and was always happy to chat. One Friday he didn't turn up, with no explanantion, which was not like him at all. I received a note next week from his wife,

knew that my oportunities were disappearing. 'I don't suppose you would be interested in coming to church next Sunday?' I ventured. 'I thought you were a Christian', he said, ' and I wondered if that was why you were so honest. Yes, I will come and I'll bring my wife and daughter. They love dressing up!'

'We have in England a particular bashfulness in everything that regards religion'
Joseph Addison

informing me that he had died suddenly of a heart attack at the age of 44 and would I come to his funeral.

I came along with a heavy heart and watched as his young wife and three daughters placed flowers on his coffin. What did Tim believe? Was faith real to him? My weekly conversations had never deepened into anything very real. Had I ever even talked to him about my faith?

The following week we had a special celebration service due to take place at our church. I had been working alongside Mark for a year and had had some good conversations about faith and business ethics. He was due to leave our work place soon and I

It was great to have Mark and his family there over the next few weeks. Sometimes we need a reminder that life is precious to prompt us into braver invitations. What do we have to lose?

'We have in England a particular bashfulness in everything that regards religion'. So wrote Joseph Addison in The Spectator in 1712. That sentiment continues to be true. We can be amazing evangelists when it comes to recommending a book or a recipe, or a favourite television programme, but enormously reticent at recommending Christianity as a lifestyle choice. Yet we know from experience how a personal relationship with the living God enriches our lives.

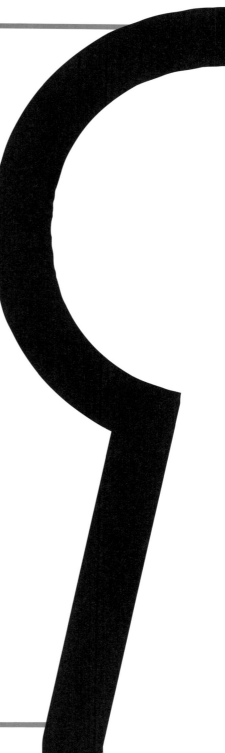

One of the saddest emotions in life must surely be regret. Often we can be sorry that we've done or not done a certain act – that's why we're so thrilled that God builds in a repentance and forgiveness clause into our relationship. To reach the latter days of your life and regret not being bolder in sharing faith with others, especially if they have died without ever hearing that message, must be hard to live with. We never know how long our life will be. Sometimes we have illusions of living forever, as Woody Allen once said, "I recently turned 60. Practically a third of my life is over."

We don't know how long we will have our friends around us either, yet we often hesitate to test the friendship by telling them what is really in our hearts. In reality it is the greatest compliment to share the secrets of our hearts with others. If someone rejects you for being real with them, then maybe you should be asking how genuine the friendship really was if they didn't actually know you very well.

We need to be bolder and not procrastinate, initiate meaningful conversations instead of engaging in superficial ones. Hopefully this book will have given you some ideas of how you can create opportunities to get alongside people and provide forums for discussion in creative, non-threatening ways. If you don't feel you can risk sounding preachy then asking questions is a good way to do it. **But do it now.**

Personal Reflection

Quality Time	Column A	Column B
Names of five best friends	1. 2. 3. 4. 5.	1. 2. 3. 4. 5.
Draw up a list of ten people you would include in a party or meal for your birthday	1. 2. 3. 4. 5. 6. 7. 8. 9. 10.	1. 2. 3. 4. 5. 6. 7. 8. 9. 10.
Last five activities / events / sports you did with friends	1. 2. 3. 4. 5.	1. 2. 3. 4. 5.

Quality Time	Column A	Column B
% of your weekday time that you spend with friends		
% of your weekend time that you spend with friends		
Community events / teams / hobbies you are involved with		
How many people do you regularly keep in touch with, maybe through letters, phone calls, texting, emails, facebook?		

Step One - Take a few moments to write down your answers, thinking about your life as a whole. Write down your responses in column A. Then go and have a cup of coffee and a bar of chocolate!

Step Two - Now, look again at the answers you wrote down and in column B transfer over just the names or activities that are non-believers or non-church activities.

How does your personal picture look? Are you surprised at how few of your good friends are non-Christians? Do you spend the majority of your time doing church activities or with other Christians? If you are spending lots of your time with those who don't know Jesus, well done! You are in a prime position to build relationships, listen, and be ready to answer for the hope that you have.

Step Three - If you are soaked in Christian friends and activities it might be time to reassess how you spend your time. How can you change? What activities can you quielty drop to make way for new opportunities? What will you do to build new opportunities into your week? When can you start?

Key Resources for
Evangelism **Today**

women actively sharing god's love

Would you like more training?

Activate Your Life

We are keen to encourage Christians to feel more confident in their personal evangelism, believing that each individual has a vital role to play in their own neighbourhood, with their own friends, work colleagues and circle of influence.

We run a website with regular updates and inspiration, as well as being active on Facebook and twitter. We organise a weekend away once a year and would love to welcome you for a time of inspiration, challenge and networking in a relaxing hotel environment. We have a small team of volunteers and are happy to travel and come and present our message to your friends, group or church. We have a power-point presentation linked to this book, which we can present to you or you can purchase to use independently. There are images from each room of a house as our little keyhole person introduces the Biblical background, relevant up to date information and throws out hundreds of ideas for reaching out. **www.activateyourlife.org.uk**

Walk Across The Room

Bill Hybels of Willow Creek church has developed a book and course that encourages individuals to build relationships, develop natural contacts and share personally. This is a testimonial approach based on trusting the guiding of the Holy Spirit and sharing friendship's transforming love. Participants are encouraged to

- offer radical acceptance and love to people God places around us

- sincerely listen and learn the life stories of friends

- envelop them in community

There is a four week course with a DVD and a guidebook that encourages individual reflection and weekly activities. Whilst it is American, the ideas and skills are easily transferable. There is a very funny section on 'how not to share your story' as well as inspiring personal tales.

www.willowcreek.com

Ready to try something NEW in a church context?

Messy Church

Started by a church in Portsmouth in 2004 with Lucy Moore this is a different way of 'doing church' and of reaching out to children and families who don't normally come. It typically includes a welcome, a long creative time to explore the Biblical theme through getting messy, a short celebration time involving story, prayer, song, and games and a sit-down meal together at tables. Ideally, all elements are for people of all ages with the aim being to introduce Jesus, to give an opportunity to encounter him and to grow closer to him.

It isn't designed just to get people to come to a regular Sunday service and it may operate as a separate congregation. Neither is it a 'quick fix'; it usually meets once a month and is a long term strategy, building relationships with families in the community rather than a one off evangelistic hit. BRF support the initiative and provide regular support material, dvds, craft boxes, books and training courses. The reputation is building and it is proving very popular, with more than 1900 Messy Churches meeting around the world. **www.messychurch.org.uk**

Sweaty Church

Pioneered by St Paul's church in York, this type of event was inspired initially by Messy Church.

This fresh expression of Church uses participation through activities, games and sport, rather than craft, as the means of families learning together. Its evocative name is earthy, entertaining, intriguing and honest. It is not hard to see why it is already drawing numbers and starting elsewhere.

Here is a type of church that connects easily with a wide variety of males and families who are missing church because of their children's sporting commitments. Just as important, Sweaty Church's 'learning by doing' approach reminds us how rare it is that the wider church caters for kinaesthetic learners, despite the legitimacy of this learning style.

The sessions are held once a month and offer high-energy games, team games and skills such as tight-rope walking and indoor hockey. Key elements are:

- a target audience of 7-11 year olds, particularly (but not exclusively) boys and their parents

- an effort to create an active and energetic space where people could engage their whole bodies in learning and worship, not just their eyes and ears

- an aim to allow Dads to enjoy the opportunity to play and learn about faith alongside their children

- teaching methods which are more interactive coaching than lecture, reinforced by themed activities

- a focus on all-age involvement, with a period where parents are gathered together for discussion over refreshments

www.sweatychurch.co.uk

'The miracle formula church leaders are hoping will reverse this religious decline... many claim Alpha has changed their lives and appear happier for the experience.' **Time Magazine**

'What distinguishes Alpha from other initiatives is the easy going, relaxed feel of the proceedings, that and its extraordinary success.' **The Times, London**

Do you have a group of friends asking questions and ready to explore deeper?

The Alpha Course

Starting out in Holy Trinity Brompton church in central London, this course was the first of its kind. Friends invite friends and almost every week there is a course running, with 800 people queueing up to come in and have an open discussion about faith, truth, reality and Jesus Christ. Twenty-two million people have done the course worldwide and it now stretches to 66,000 courses in 169 countries in 112 languages. There is Alpha running for students, youth, in the workplace, for Forces, for prisons, for seniors, in a catholic context, for ESOL.

Many of the people now running the Alpha organisation came to faith through this course. Tricia Neal, the head of Alpha International, believes that friendship evangelism is key to the success of the course, 'friends bring friends'. The best marketeers who usually get the most succesful invitations to each course, are those who have just completed it for the first time. The course takes time to explore the meaning of life, who Jesus is and the work of the Holy Spirit. It works with a DVD or a talk and time to discuss the issues in small groups. Alpha works - lives are changed!

www.alpha.org

Christianity Explored

Christianity Explored originated in All Souls Church, Langham Place, London. It focuses in on the gospel of Mark and takes group participants in seven weeks through key questions linked to the story of Jesus. There is a set of videos featuring author Rico Tice and booklets for each person, as well as a group leader's guide. The videos are well presented with lots of good locations and background images. Key questions addressed are:

- Good News - What are we doing here?
- Identity - Who is Jesus?
- Sin - Why did Jesus come?
- The cross - Why did Jesus die?
- Resurrection - Why did Jesus rise?
- Grace - How can God accept us?
- Come and Die -What does it mean?

The course assumes an awareness of God and the authority of the Bible. It is particularly good at exploring grace and the video for week six is very moving.

There is a follow on course called Discipleship Explored which delves deeper and is designed for those who want to make the most of their Christianity. It looks at the book of Philippians during eight weeks and has a dvd with Barry Cooper.

www.christianityexplored.org

"TWENTY YEARS FROM NOW YOU'LL BE MORE DISAPPOINTED BY THE THINGS THAT YOU DIDN'T DO THAN BY THE ONES YOU DID.

SO THROW OFF THE BOWLINES, SAIL AWAY FROM THE SAFE HARBOUR, CATCH THE TRADE WINDS IN YOUR SAILS.

EXPLORE. DREAM. DISCOVER"

Mark Twain

Notes:

Notes: